My older children love this with taco sauce and tortilla chips!

½   cup low-salt canned kidney beans
    —rinsed and drained
¾   lb. lean ground beef
1   slice whole wheat bread—torn
1   small carrot—finely grated
1   egg
2   tbsp. finely chopped onion
1   tbsp. diced mild green chilis
1   tbsp. salt-free tomato paste
1   small clove garlic—minced or pressed
2   tsp. apple juice concentrate
1   tsp. dijon mustard
1   tsp. chili powder
½   tsp. dried thyme
¼   tsp. low sodium soy sauce

Preheat cookie sheet in oven to 350°. Mash or chop kidney beans and place in a medium bowl. Add the remaining ingredients. Knead until well combined. Press into 2–4 (depending on size) mini loaf pans about ¾ full. Place on cookie sheet in oven and bake for approximately 40 minutes or until no longer pink in the middles. Spoon off fat from tops and allow to cool. Serve sliced or in cubes. May be frozen.

Food For Little Fingers

Victoria Jenest

St. Martin's Paperbacks

FOOD FOR LITTLE FINGERS

Copyright © 1997 by Victoria Jenest.

Cover photograph by Peter Brandt.

ISBN: 0-312-96097-2

Printed in the United States of America

St. Martin's Paperbacks edition/January 1997

10 9 8 7 6 5 4 3 2 1

To my beautiful children Brandon, Garrett and Mackenzie, who are the reason these recipes exist. May they be one ingredient in the foundation on which you build healthy, happy lives.

Contents

Acknowledgments

I'd like to thank the following friends and family members for their enthusiasm and support of this book:

Pat Wingenroth and Wendi Deaner, who threw me a party for *finishing* the manuscript!

Bron Savage, one of my oldest and "bestest" friends, for taking writing classes with me back in high school, and for having another baby just so she could test my recipes (yeah, right!).

Lyz Vogel, for offering her artistic abilities every time I had a new "brilliant idea"—even though none ever came to fruition!

Anthony Marsh, for getting his books published right around the same time as mine and empathizing with me through the whole process!

My huge and loving family: Fred and Laura Whitefield, Linda Whitefield, Steve Whitefield, Jeff Whitefield, Ken and Maji Irvin, Gayle Jenest, Mike and Lori Garon, Harvey Milstein and Lane Rieck.

My agent, David Hendlin, for his patience and perseverance.

Jennifer Weis, my editor at St. Martin's Press, for donating her baby for the cover!

My perfect husband, Mark, for typing the manuscript on our very slow word processor (no, we don't have a computer, yet); for being my proofreader, recipe title consultant and best friend. Without his support throughout *and* his infinite "enthusiasm" during the taste testing phase of this book, I don't think I would have finished it.

Finally, to my Grandma Frances, who was my inspiration. Wherever she is now, I know she must be cooking!

Food
For
Little
Fingers

Foreword

Eleven years ago, when my first baby was born, I promised myself that sugar, salt and white flour would never touch his lips. Keeping that promise was easy while he was eating out of baby food jars; all I had to do was read the labels and make sure the ingredients were to my liking. But, when he reached the finger food stage, easy meals became a thing of the past. I learned that even innocent looking ketchup had salt and sugar in it! Suddenly, I was severely limited, and when we were both bored with peas and Cheerios, I knew that I had to get creative.

Growing up in a Jewish household, food was always center stage. From the time I could walk, I followed my grandmother around the kitchen seeping up delicious aromas and a love for cooking. Many years later, my grandmother became ill and I was chosen as her guardian. It was my turn to become the cook, which was a challenge because my grandmother was a diabetic and on a strict diet. This experience would later become invaluable when I was faced with feeding my children.

So, with my grandmother as my inspiration and my son as my guinea pig, I set out to devise salt-, sugar- and white flour-free recipes so that we would never be bored again! Since my son was not yet adept at using a spoon, I made all of the recipes of the *finger food* variety so that some food would actually make it into his mouth!

Eleven years and 2 children later, I had many recipes "under my apron," so to speak. I kept most of these recipes on tiny pieces of tattered paper strewn around my kitchen until I realized that maybe other parents would benefit from my many hours spent experimenting in the kitchen. And that is how my book was born!

Introduction

Parents today are being inundated with helpful advice on how to feed their babies. If you buy different baby nutrition books, they will most likely contradict one another in at least one area. Probably, the most consistent recommendation is to avoid feeding sugar to babies and toddlers. Nevertheless, many of these books include recipes which contain other sweeteners such as honey, brown sugar, molasses and/or maple syrup which are essentially the same as sugar (or sucrose). A large intake of sugar, especially if started at a young age, may result in obesity and tooth decay. It has also been linked to hyperactivity and diabetes. These are *facts* that relate to all of the above-mentioned sweeteners.

Another area of concern is the consumption of salt. While everyone needs salt in their diet, the foods we eat every day (bread, cheese, milk, etc.) contain enough to meet our needs (and a baby's) either by naturally containing sodium or by having it as an additive. Heavy salt users tend to be more prone to heart attacks, strokes, high blood pressure, and weight gain. Beyond taste, there is no reason to add salt to our already sodium laden diets—and especially not to a baby's!

3

In the area of whole wheat flour vs. white flour, I don't think any nutritionist or pediatrician would argue that whole wheat, or any whole grain flour, is preferable to white flour which has most of its nutrients removed during the processing. Unlike whole grain flour, the white variety also offers no fiber, which is an extremely important part of our diets. Eating a high fiber diet can help prevent constipation and obesity. It has also been associated with the prevention of colon cancer.

This recipe book is designed to be used in conjunction with any nutrition books that you already own and trust. It is also intended for parents who want their children to remain sugar-, salt- and white flour-free for as long as possible. We all know that eventually our children will be introduced to these ingredients by a friend or maybe even as a special treat by us; but the longer they remain free of these unnecessary additives, the less likely they will be to require them. This not only keeps them healthy now but contributes to a much healthier adult!

1

Why Only Finger Food Recipes?

1. Around the age of 1, babies start developing a sense of independence. With this blossoming independence, babies will usually prefer (if not demand) to feed themselves. A spoon is a wonderful concept; but for toddlers it's more of a toy than a utensil. Encourage children to practice with spoons and forks; but if you want significantly more food to make it into their mouths, letting them use their fingers is the preferred method.
2. They allow babies to eat at their own pace.
3. Babies can practice hand/eye coordination and pincher grip.
4. They allow Mom or Dad to have their hands free to do something else such as the dishes, eat a meal of their own or do a song and dance for baby!

A FEW WORDS ABOUT UTENSILS

I'll never forget the first time my daughter "speared" her first pea. She held up her fork with the one pea dangling precariously on the end and gave me a look of gratifying accomplishment. I knew instantly that it was the same pea she had been "chasing" for the past ten minutes! She popped the pea into her mouth and proceeded to use her fork as a comb just like Ariel did in *The Little Mermaid*! I guess she figured one pea every ten minutes just wasn't worth the effort, and this funny shaped item had much better uses!

For babies in the 10 month–2 year age group, forks and spoons are usually used not so much for eating but as sling shots to fling food around your kitchen and sometimes at you! Does that mean you should never give your child a fork or spoon? Of course not! I assume Ariel eventually learned to use her fork correctly.

Forks and spoons (hopefully, you don't even own a "baby" knife!) should be introduced as soon as your baby is sitting in a high chair. Preferably, they should have short handles and dull tines on the forks. As to when they will actually be used is up to your baby and will depend on his manual dexterity and experience. I still catch my ten-year-old eating his steak like a caveman and picking up his macaroni with his fingers. I think it is just instinct—who doesn't prefer to use their hands to eat chicken rather than a fork and knife? After all, we were eating with our fingers for thousands of years before flatware was introduced in the late Middle Ages!

Since it is such a learned skill, it will take some rehearsals to master. So let your baby see you and the family using your utensils and give her some of her own to fiddle with. She may not get any food into her mouth but after some practice she will use it at least part-time. Meanwhile, keep serving finger foods (most can also be eaten with a fork or spoon) so when frustration sets in, she'll have something she can really sink her fingers into!

2

Tips for Using This Book

These recipes are intended for babies who are eating a variety of foods (usually by about 10 months) and are accustomed to finger foods. If you are in doubt, check with your pediatrician.

In order to use this book to its full potential, you should own these kitchen utensils:

Non-stick fry pan: A non-stick pan will cut down on the amount of fat required for cooking or frying.

Food processor or strong blender

Plastic airtight containers and/or bags

Individual casserole dishes

Steamer basket: Steaming foods rather than boiling them helps to retain their vitamins. (See Chapter 9)

Miniature loaf pans

1 quart square or rectangular baking or casserole dish

A lot of patience and a big washcloth!

Be aware of the choking hazards to babies and toddlers. For babies with no teeth or only the front teeth (not for chewing), the foods to refrain from feeding are:

Uncooked raisins
Whole peas
Hard fruits such as apples and unripe pears, peaches, etc.
Nuts
Meat or poultry that hasn't been ground
Uncooked carrot
Whole grapes
Hot dogs (Not only are these a choking hazard, but they also contain nitrates and are not healthful for children)
Popcorn
Hard candies (you should know how I feel about these!)
Peanut Butter (can cause gagging if not thinned out)
Basically, anything hard that cannot be "gummed" into mush or that doesn't dissolve in the mouth should not be offered to babies without teeth (or with only the front teeth)

For babies with molars, you can introduce:

Fresh soft raisins
Apples and other hard fruits sliced very thin
Halved grapes
Very tender meat and poultry

Children don't learn how to properly use their teeth until around 2–3 years of age, so until that time, if in doubt, don't offer it.

I will indicate with an asterisk (*) which recipes are only intended for older toddlers with molars.

Don't let your baby eat lying down or walking around. A sudden fall or jolt could cause her to "inhale" her food.

Always be present while baby is eating and know how to perform the Heimlich maneuver in case of a choking incident.

Don't condescend to a baby's taste buds! Some of these recipes are very sophisticated, and you might hesitate to give them to your baby. But I assure you, babies can enjoy green chili peppers just like adults—and many do! Remember, in other cultures babies grow up on a multitude of foods, including some spicy dishes, that even some adults in *our* society would balk at. Which leads me to this . . .

Starting babies on a variety of foods early in their lives will help them retain their diverse tastes as they grow.

If your baby is prone to food allergies, be aware of some of these common culprits:

Egg whites: You can substitute 2 egg yolks for
      every whole egg asked for in a recipe
Berries
Tomatoes
Wheat: You can substitute another whole grain
      flour in recipes calling for whole wheat flour
      such as oat, barley or rice.

Peas and beans: With most recipes, you can exclude
these ingredients
Nuts: Again, simply exclude them.

Try to use fresh or frozen foods instead of
canned. The canning process depletes most of the
vitamins.

I have made these recipes with regular baking
powder which is high in sodium. If you can find the
low-sodium version (it's available at most health
food stores) then substitute it by increasing the low-
sodium baking powder by ½ tsp. for every tsp. of the
regular. For example if a recipe calls for 1 tsp. regular, substitute 1½ tsp. low sodium.

Read labels! When buying food always read the
ingredient list. Ingredients are listed in order of
their quantity. The FDA (Food and Drug Adminis-
tration) has passed a regulation that all foods must
have nutritional guidelines on their packaging.
They must list the fiber, sugar and sodium content
among other things. This may not make it as fun to
eat a candy bar knowing it has 12 grams of fat, but
it certainly helps when you're shopping for your
family!

Many of these recipes call for whole wheat bread.
When shopping for bread for your baby, make sure
you read the ingredients. Most whole wheat breads
sold at your local market contain some form of sugar
(remember corn syrup, honey and molasses are all
forms of sugar). If you must buy one of these, make
sure the sugar is low on the ingredient list. Also,
many commercial breads are not whole wheat.

Make sure the first ingredient is whole wheat flour or stone ground whole wheat (enriched wheat and unbleached wheat, while healthier than bleached white flour, are still not whole wheat). I have included a recipe for whole grain bread for those of you who prefer to make your own.

A few of these recipes call for whole wheat bread crumbs. These can be purchased at a health food store or you can make your own by placing slices of whole wheat bread on the center rack in a preheated 300° oven. Bake for 20 minutes then spin in your blender or food processor until fine. Bread crumbs can be stored in an airtight container in your freezer. One slice of bread makes approximately ¼ cup bread crumbs.

Don't judge by appearances. Without the limitations that your sight and taste impose, you can make endless possibilities for your baby! And speaking of taste . . .

By all means, sample these dishes—you might enjoy them! But don't use your taste buds as a flavor barometer. Most likely, yours have been trained to enjoy foods with added salt and sugar. Remember, your baby's taste buds are a blank slate, and she can't miss what she's never had.

Don't feed your baby the same food every day. Most children will get "peanut butter and jelly syndrome" (that or another food is all they'll eat) at one time or another. You can significantly reduce the chance of this happening by varying your baby's diet.

When trying these recipes, make sure you offer them to your baby on at least two occasions. Babies are fickle. Though she may dislike something one day, she may develop a taste for it the next day.

If babies take more than one bite of anything, you can usually assume that they like it. If after a few bites she stops eating, don't be upset or try to force her to eat (good luck with that concept!). She's probably full, and it's best simply to remove her from the high chair. A baby will always eat enough to survive. If she misses one meal, you can be certain that she will make up for it at the next! Keep in mind that a baby's appetite drops substantially around the first birthday due to a slower growth rate.

I have designed these recipes to be made with the smallest quantities possible. This way there is less waste if baby decides a recipe is not for her. As a result, some of these recipes call for 1/4 to 3/4 pounds of ground meat. Unfortunately, meat usually isn't packaged in these increments. My suggestion is to buy a pound and divide it into quarter pounds before freezing. This way, you defrost only what you need. If your baby has a favorite, double the recipe.

I will indicate which recipes may be frozen. This is an added convenience which allows you to cook less frequently, and simply defrost previously prepared meals.

When I refer to fruit juice concentrate in a recipe, I'm speaking of the frozen variety that has been defrosted. In some recipes where it will be cooked or used in a beverage, defrosting is unnecessary.

Most of the ingredients in these recipes can be found at your local grocery store. If you can't find a specific item, check the diet and nutrition aisle. If it's not there, check with the nearest health food store.

Don't cook or store acidic food (such as tomato sauce) in aluminum foil or pans. The food may absorb the aluminum.

Try to use stone-ground whole wheat flour. Vitamins are sometimes ground out by the steel grinders that are used for regular whole wheat flour. If you prefer oat flour, make your own by grinding quick cooking oats in a blender or food processor.

If you have access to whole wheat pastry flour, substitute it for the whole wheat flour in recipes for pancakes, muffins and cookies.

These recipes are designed to be easy to grasp by little fingers, but if you or your baby are uncomfortable eating with your fingers, then by all means grab a fork!

If your baby is too young to eat fresh onions, then simply substitute ¼ tsp. onion powder for every tablespoon of fresh onion called for in a recipe.

If you have a hard time cleaning your baby's face, try this. When it's time for me to clean up my baby, I play "I'm gonna get you!" I keep repeating this phrase and then "attacking" her face with the washcloth; wiping as I do so. She still moves around so it takes a few tries, but, at least, she's laughing instead of getting upset about having her face washed.

Let your baby get messy! Babies are stain-resistant, unlike their surroundings. So, cover the floor with plastic or newspaper and allow them to learn, play and get messy. It's all part of their dining experience!

VITAMINS AND MINERALS ESSENTIAL TO YOUR CHILD'S GROWTH

VITAMIN A—For healthy eyes, skin, teeth and digestive tract. Necessary for growth.
FIND VITAMIN A IN . . . Dark green vegetables such as broccoli and spinach. Deep yellow and orange vegetables such as carrots, pumpkin, sweet potatoes and winter squashes. Fruits such as oranges, tomatoes, apricots, peaches, cantaloupe, strawberries, papaya and watermelons. Liver, lentils, butter, whole milk and eggs.

VITAMIN B$_1$ (THIAMINE)—Encourages good appetite and digestion. Keeps nervous system healthy.
FIND VITAMIN B$_1$ IN . . . Liver, pork, poultry, fish, nuts, milk, dried peas and beans, whole grain breads and potatoes.

VITAMIN B$_2$ (RIBOFLAVIN)—For healthy skin and eyes. Helps cells convert food into energy.
FIND VITAMIN B$_2$ IN . . . Whole grain breads, meat, liver, milk, green leafy vegetables and eggs.

VITAMIN B$_3$ (NIACIN)—Encourages healthy skin, digestive tract, tongue, nervous system and normal growth. Assists body cells in obtaining energy from food.

FIND VITAMIN B_3 IN . . . Liver, fish, meat, peanuts, yeast, whole grain breads, beans and peas.

VITAMIN B_{12}—Encourages body cells to function normally. Essential for formation of red blood cells.

FIND VITAMIN B_{12} IN . . . Liver, kidney, milk and milk products, fish, eggs, meat and shellfish.

VITAMIN C (ASCORBIC ACID)—Helps form bones, teeth and cartilage. Assists in wound healing and promotes the absorption of iron.

FIND VITAMIN C IN . . . Green peppers, parsley, broccoli, brussels sprouts, strawberries, citrus fruits, guava, cabbage, potatoes, green leafy vegetables, tomatoes, cantaloupe, blueberries and papaya.

VITAMIN D—Regulates proper growth of bones and teeth.

FIND VITAMIN D IN . . . The sun, (our skin absorbs it from the sunlight) oily fish such as tuna and salmon, egg yolk, yeast, margarine, liver and fortified milk.

VITAMIN E—Protects red blood cells, encourages normal growth patterns and is essential for proper digestion of unsaturated fatty acids.

FIND VITAMIN E IN . . . Asparagus, peanuts, vegetable oils, wheat germ, broccoli, cabbage, whole grains and margarine.

CALCIUM—Helps to build strong bones and teeth. Helps blood to clot.

FIND CALCIUM IN . . . Milk and dairy products, broccoli and legumes.

IRON—Combines with protein to make healthy blood. Prevents anemia.

FIND IRON IN . . . Dried beans and peas, dark green leafy vegetables, whole grain breads and cereals, liver, meat, egg yolk and dried fruit.

MAGNESIUM—Regulates cell metabolism and growth. Activates several enzymes.

FIND MAGNESIUM IN . . . Legumes, nuts, whole grains, bananas, milk, meat and most dark green vegetables.

POTASSIUM—Encourages growth and muscle strength. Helps regulate water in the body.

FIND POTASSIUM IN . . . Bananas, dried dates, cantaloupe, meat, milk, citrus fruits, dark green leafy vegetables, apricots, tomato juice, broccoli, potatoes, peanuts, squashes, orange juice and wheat germ.

ZINC—Aids growth, healing wounds and helps prevent anemia.

FIND ZINC IN . . . Breast milk, shellfish, dried beans and peas, nuts, whole grains, meat, cheese, liver and eggs.

SODIUM—Yes, I said sodium! We *do* need sodium in our diets to help regulate the water in our bodies and to balance the acid base.

FIND SODIUM IN . . . Almost everything! Sodium occurs naturally in an abundance of food. So much so, that there is no need to *add* it to anything (via table salt).

I have tried to include most of the above-mentioned foods in my recipes so that your child will get a variety of the vitamins and minerals that are so important to her!

3

Meals-in-One

In this chapter, I have included recipes that contain substantial quantities of food from at least 3 of the 4 food groups. Nutritionally, these are optimum for babies and toddlers and are the ultimate in convenience for parents. There is only 1 course to prepare! Because of their simplicity, they are perfect to leave for Grandma or the babysitter.

Most of these recipes can be frozen and simply defrosted in a microwave or in a refrigerator overnight. I suggest cutting the meatloaves into serving sizes before freezing. This way you only defrost as much as you need.

MUNCHKIN MEATLOAVES

Your little munchkin will love this traditional (but healthier) meatloaf. Older children, Mom and Dad can even make sandwiches out of the leftovers—just like the bigger version!

1	egg
1/3	cup milk, breast milk or formula
1/4	cup whole wheat fine dry bread crumbs
1/4	cup shredded carrot
1	tbsp. snipped parsley
1/4	tsp. onion powder
1/4	tsp. ground sage
3/4	lb. lean ground meat
	(beef, chicken, turkey, etc.)
3	tbsp. salt-free tomato paste
2	tbsp. apple juice concentrate

Preheat oven to 350°. Beat together egg and milk in a medium mixing bowl. Stir in bread crumbs, carrot, parsley, onion powder and sage. Add ground meat and blend well. Press into 2–3 (depending on size) mini loaf pans about 3/4 full. Bake for 40 minutes or until meat is no longer pink in the middle. Remove from oven and spoon off excess fat.

Mix tomato paste and apple juice concentrate together. Spread over the tops of the loaves. Return to oven and continue cooking 15 minutes. Allow to cool, remove from pans and cut into serving size pieces. May be frozen.

MINI TURKEY LOAVES

A great way to sneak spinach into the diet! It makes plain meatloaf look a lot more colorful too!

1/2	lb. ground turkey
1	egg
1/4	cup milk, breast milk or formula
2	slices whole wheat bread torn into soft crumbs
1/2	small onion, finely chopped
5	oz. frozen chopped spinach, defrosted and squeezed dry
2	tsp. dijon mustard
1/2	tsp. dried basil
1/4	tsp. dried thyme
1/4	tsp. dried oregano

Preheat a cookie sheet in oven to 350°. Combine all ingredients in a medium mixing bowl. Knead with hands until well combined. Spread into 2–3 (depending on size) mini loaf pans about 3/4 full. Place in oven on cookie sheet and bake approximately 40 minutes or until meat is no longer pink in the middle. Spoon off fat from tops, allow to cool and cut into serving size pieces. May be frozen.

MACKENZIE'S MEATLOAF

This is my daughter's favorite meatloaf so I decided to give it her name!

½	lb. zucchini, grated
½	lb. lean ground meat (beef, chicken, turkey, etc.)
1	cup fresh coarsely torn whole wheat bread (about 1 slice)
1	egg
¼	cup shredded jack cheese
1½	tbsp. salt-free tomato paste
2	tsp. chopped fresh parsley
¼	tsp. dried basil

Preheat cookie sheet in oven to 350°. Combine all ingredients in a medium mixing bowl. Knead with fingers until well combined. Press into 2–4 (depending on size) mini loaf pans about ¾ full. Bake on cookie sheet approximately 40 minutes or until no longer pink in the middles. Spoon off fat from the tops and allow to cool. Cut into slices or cubes to serve. May be frozen.

MINI-MEX MEATLOAVES

My older children love this with taco sauce and tortilla chips!

1/2	cup low-salt canned kidney beans, rinsed and drained
3/4	lb. lean ground beef
1	slice whole wheat bread, coarsely torn
1	small carrot, finely grated
1	egg
2	tbsp. finely chopped onion
1	tbsp. diced mild green chilis
1	tbsp. salt-free tomato paste
1	small clove garlic, minced or pressed
2	tsp. apple juice concentrate
1	tsp. dijon mustard
1	tsp. chili powder
1/2	tsp. dried thyme
1/4	tsp. low sodium soy sauce

Preheat cookie sheet in oven to 350°. Mash or chop kidney beans and place in a medium bowl. Add the remaining ingredients. Knead until well combined. Press into 2–4 (depending on size) mini loaf pans about 3/4 full. Place on cookie sheet in oven and bake for approximately 40 minutes or until no longer pink in the middles. Spoon off fat from tops and allow to cool. Serve sliced or in cubes. May be frozen.

BABY BURGERS

Just like Mom and Dad's but a lot healthier!

½	lb. lean ground meat (beef, chicken, turkey, etc.)
2	small carrots, finely grated
½	cup dry baby cereal (rice, oatmeal, etc.) or fine dry whole wheat bread crumbs
1	egg
¼	tsp. onion or garlic powder

Mix all of the above ingredients in a medium bowl until well combined. Form into 4 balls, then press thin with palm to make patties. Cook patties in a non-stick skillet over low-medium heat approximately 5 minutes per side or until patties are no longer pink in the middle. Allow to cool and serve whole or in pieces. May be frozen.

MEAT AND POTATO PATTIES

Only for the most "down to earth" toddlers!

1	small white rose potato
½	cup raisins
1	egg
¼	cup shelled walnut pieces
1	tbsp. fresh parsley
½	lb. lean ground beef
½	cup fine whole wheat bread crumbs

Cut unpeeled potato into quarters. Boil, covered in 1 quart water 15–20 minutes or until tender. During last 10 minutes add the raisins to the water. When potatoes are soft and raisins are plump, drain the water.

In a food processor or blender, grind together the raisins, potato, egg, walnuts and parsley. Remove to a bowl and stir in the meat and bread crumbs. Mix well.

With wet hands, shape into 6 balls and press flat with palm of hand to make patties. Fry over low heat in a non-stick skillet on both sides until browned and cooked through. Allow to cool and serve whole or in pieces. May be frozen.

TUNA PATTY CAKES

Patty cake, patty cake, fisherman . . . make me some protein as fast as you can.

6   oz. can low sodium tuna in water,
     well drained and flaked*
1/2 cup fine dry whole wheat bread crumbs
1/4 cup frozen chopped spinach,
     defrosted and squeezed dry
1   tsp. minced onion
1/4 tsp. garlic powder
1/4 cup milk, breast milk or formula

Mix together the tuna, bread crumbs, spinach, onion, and garlic powder. Add milk and blend until mixture is moist, using more milk if necessary. Form into 6–8 small patties. Broil on each side for about 5 minutes or until browned. Cool and serve whole or in pieces. May be frozen.

*This is usually found in the diet aisle of the grocery store.

GERMY MEATBALLS

These go together so easily and freeze well. Babies love to eat them plain; but for a meal the whole family can enjoy, add them to your favorite spaghetti sauce and serve over pasta.

½   lb. lean ground beef
½   cup wheat germ
1   small zucchini, grated
1   egg
1   tsp. Italian seasoning
½   tsp. garlic powder

Mix together all ingredients in a medium bowl. Knead with hands until well combined. Form into 1-inch meatballs.

Fill a medium skillet with 1 inch of water and bring to a boil. Drop in meatballs. Bring to a boil again, lower heat and simmer 5 minutes or until cooked through. Drain water and allow meatballs to cool. Serve whole or cut in half. May be frozen.

ME SO YUNG MEATBALLS

An Asian meal and an Italian tradition all "rolled" into one!

½	lb. lean ground pork
¼	lb. lean ground beef
1	small zucchini, shredded
1	egg
¼	cup quick cooking oats
⅓	cup low or no sodium chicken broth*
2	tbsp. minced onion
2	tsp. sesame seeds
2	tsp. low-sodium soy sauce
½	tsp. ground ginger
1	small clove garlic, pressed or mashed

Preheat oven to 450°. Combine all ingredients in a medium mixing bowl. Knead until well combined. Form into 1-inch balls. Place meatballs without touching on a rimmed cookie sheet. Cover loosely with aluminum foil so it isn't touching meatballs. Bake for 30 minutes or until cooked through. Allow to cool. Serve whole or cut in half. May be frozen.

*Check the label to make sure the chicken broth does not contain MSG. Health Valley makes a great no salt/no MSG brand. Look for it in the soup or diet sections of your grocery store.

CHICKY CHEESE SHELLS*

Okay . . . so a certain mouse had nothing to do with this recipe, but just mention the familiar sounding name and most kids will at least try it!

3	oz. giant pasta shells
5	oz. frozen chopped broccoli, defrosted and drained
2	tsp. margarine
1	green onion, chopped
1/2	cup chopped mushrooms
1	tsp. dried basil
1	tsp. dried oregano
2	tsp. whole wheat flour
1/3	cup milk
1/2	cup cooked shredded chicken
1/2	cup shredded mozzarella or jack cheese
1/4	cup grated Parmesan cheese
1/4	cup milk

Cook pasta according to package directions. Rinse with cold water, drain and set aside.

Preheat oven to 375°. Melt the margarine in a medium non-stick skillet. Add the onions, mushrooms, basil, oregano and broccoli. Stir and add flour. Pour in 1/3 cup milk. Heat to boiling; stirring constantly until mixture thickens. Stir in chicken, cheese and half the Parmesan.

Fill the pasta shells with the broccoli mixture and place in a greased 1 quart casserole dish in a single layer. Sprinkle with the remaining Parmesan cheese and then drizzle with the 1/4 cup milk. Bake covered for 15 minutes or until heated through. May be frozen.

*This is for toddlers with molars.

COCKLE SHELLS

This is a perfect meal-in-one, even for a vegetarian child.

6	oz. giant pasta shells
1/2	lb. soft tofu, rinsed, drained and cut into cubes
5	oz. frozen chopped spinach, rinsed and squeezed dry
1/2	cup shredded mozzarella cheese
2	tbsp. grated Parmesan cheese
1	tbsp. onion, finely chopped
1	clove garlic
1	tsp. Italian seasoning
	dash pepper
8	oz. can salt-free tomato sauce

Cook shells according to package directions. Rinse with cold water and drain. Set aside.

Preheat oven to 350°. In a medium mixing bowl, combine the tofu, spinach, mozzarella cheese, Parmesan cheese, onion, garlic, Italian seasoning and pepper. Mix well.

Spread a thin layer of tomato sauce in a 1 quart casserole dish. Fill each shell with the tofu mixture and place in a single layer in the dish. Pour remaining tomato sauce evenly over the shells. Bake, uncovered, 30–35 minutes or until heated through. Allow to cool and serve whole or cut into pieces. Separate into individual servings before freezing.

GREEN CHEESE SQUARES

This is another great vegetarian meal.

2	tsp. olive oil
$1/2$	small onion, finely chopped
1	small clove garlic, minced or pressed
10	oz. box frozen chopped spinach, thawed and squeezed dry
$3/4$	cup cooked brown rice ($1/4$ cup uncooked)
$1/2$	cup shredded jack cheese
2	eggs
$1/4$	cup chopped fresh parsley
2	tbsp. fine dry whole wheat bread crumbs
1	tbsp. grated Parmesan cheese
$1/4$	tsp. dried thyme

Preheat oven to 375°. Rub a 1 quart square or rectangular casserole dish with 1 tsp. of the olive oil. Heat the remaining oil in a medium non-stick skillet over medium-high heat. Add the onion and garlic. Sauté a few minutes until limp and slightly brown. Add the spinach. Remove from heat and stir. Transfer to a large mixing bowl. Add the rice, jack cheese, eggs, parsley, bread crumbs, Parmesan cheese and thyme. Stir until well combined. Press into the casserole dish and bake 20–25 minutes or until set. Allow to cool and cut into squares. May be frozen.

PASGETTI PIE

Babies usually love the taste of pasta but the spaghetti shape is a little more difficult to get into the mouth. This is a different way to use spaghetti while making it a little easier to handle!

1   tsp. olive oil, divided in half
3   eggs
8   oz. cottage cheese
¼   cup Parmesan cheese
¼   tsp. dried basil
2   cups well-cooked whole wheat spaghetti
    (approximately 2 oz. uncooked)
½   cup chopped mushrooms
½   cup cooked chicken or turkey,
    chopped fine or ground
¼   cup finely chopped onion
1   small clove garlic, minced or pressed
½   cup chopped fresh spinach

Preheat oven to 400°. Rub a 1–1½ quart square or rectangular casserole dish with ½ tsp. olive oil. Set aside.

Beat the eggs in a medium mixing bowl. Add the cottage cheese, Parmesan cheese and basil. Stir well.

Chop the spaghetti and stir into egg mixture. Set aside.

Heat the remaining olive oil in a medium non-stick skillet. Add the mushrooms, chicken, onion, and garlic until vegetables are limp and meat is browned. Add the spinach and sauté 2 minutes more. Drain. Add the vegetable mixture to egg mixture and stir well. Spread into casserole dish. Bake 25 minutes or until set. Allow to cool and cut into squares. May be frozen.

QUICHES AND HUGS

Don't forget the hugs. They are the most important ingredient!

Crust:

1½ cups mashed potatoes (approximately 2
    medium potatoes)
2   tbsp. minced onion

Filling:

¼   cup shredded jack cheese
¼   cup shredded cheddar cheese
¼   cup cooked chicken, finely chopped or ground
¼   cup chopped cooked broccoli
¼   cup grated carrot
2   small eggs
¼   cup milk, breast milk or formula

Preheat oven to 350°. Mix together the mashed potatoes and onion. Press along bottom and sides of a greased 6 cup muffin tin to make shells. Bake in oven for 20 minutes. Remove, but leave oven on.

In a medium mixing bowl, mix together the jack and cheddar cheeses, chicken and veggies. Evenly press into each potato cup.

Beat together the eggs and milk. Pour evenly over potato cups. Return to oven and bake for 25 minutes or until knife inserted in centers comes out clean. Allow to cool and remove from pan. Cut into quarters and serve. May be frozen.

TINY TOT TAMALE PIES

A mild "south of the border" taste that will definitely turn your baby into a multi-cultural connoisseur!

For easier eating, cut the tamales into quarters before serving.

1½ cups cold water
¾ cup cornmeal
¼ cup shredded carrots
¼ lb. lean ground meat (beef, turkey, chicken, etc.)
¼ cup shredded cheddar or American cheese
⅛ tsp. onion powder
⅛ tsp. garlic powder
½ cup low sodium canned kidney beans, rinsed and drained
vegetable spray

Preheat oven to 350°. Spray a 12-cup muffin tin with vegetable spray. In a small saucepan, combine water and cornmeal. Cook and stir over medium heat until mixture is very thick and stiff (5–10 minutes). Remove from heat and allow to cool. Meanwhile, cook ground meat and carrots in skillet, breaking meat into tiny pieces. When meat is brown, remove from heat and drain fat. Add cheese, onion powder and garlic powder, stirring until cheese melts. Puree, chop or mash kidney beans. Add to meat mixture and stir well.

Reserve ⅓ of the cornmeal mixture. With the other ⅔, press along bottom and sides of muffin cups. Spoon 1 heaping tbsp. of meat mixture into each cup. Spread remaining ⅓ cornmeal over meat mixture in each cup. Seal edges with fingers. Bake

for 15 minutes. Allow to cool and remove from pan.
May be frozen.

EMERALD PILLOWS

*This is adapted from my grandmother's favorite
"Kreplach" recipe. A "Kreplach" is a stuffed triangu-
lar shaped dumpling that usually floats in soup.
These were always my favorite as a child. "Sans"
soup, they make a perfect finger food.*

*It may take a little extra effort to make them, but
they freeze and reheat perfectly, so make a big batch.*

Dough:
³/₄   cup chopped frozen spinach,
      defrosted and squeezed only semi-dry
1   egg
1¼   cups whole wheat flour

To make dough: In blender or food processor, combine the spinach and egg. Blend until smooth.
Transfer to a large mixing bowl. Add the whole
wheat flour; using more if needed to form a stiff
dough. Transfer to floured surface. Knead for about
1 minute. Using a rolling pin, roll dough as thin as
possible without breaking it. Let sit while you prepare a filling (see recipes below). Cut round edges off
to form a large square. Cut into 2-inch squares using
a sharp knife or pizza cutter. Remaining dough may
be rolled out to make more squares.

Drop a teaspoon of filling into center of each
square. Fold over one corner to form a triangle. Seal
edges with a wet finger. Cook in boiling water 5 minutes or until triangles have floated to the top. With
a slotted spoon, transfer to bowl of cold water, allow
to cool and serve. Remaining triangles may be

frozen. To reheat, cook in boiling water as directed above.

Fillings:

CHICKEN LIVER:
½	cup chicken livers
1	tsp. vegetable oil
2	hard cooked egg yolks
1	tsp. onion powder

Cook livers in oil in a small non-stick skillet 8 minutes or until no longer pink. Transfer to blender or food processor. Add egg yolks and onion powder. Grind until smooth.

CHICKEN:
1	cup pureed cooked chicken*
	or 4 jars chicken baby food
1	egg
1	small carrot, finely grated
2	tsp. chopped fresh parsley
1	tsp. onion powder

Mix all ingredients together in a medium bowl.

*To grind chicken: Boil 1 lb. boneless, skinless chicken breasts, thighs or combination of both in large saucepan of water for approximately 30 minutes or until cooked through. Drain, saving broth. Transfer to blender or food processor. Add 3 tbsp. broth and grind adding more broth if needed.

LOS NIÑOS' TURNOVERS

Don't be intimidated by the fact that this recipe has chili powder in it. It adds flavor—not heat. You'll be surprised at how your baby will gobble them up!

¼	lb. lean ground beef
½	small carrot, grated
1	small clove garlic, minced or pressed
½	tsp. onion powder
1	tbsp. unsalted tomato sauce
½	tsp. chili powder
¼	cup low sodium canned kidney beans, rinsed and drained
3	slices whole wheat bread chili powder

Preheat oven to 350°. In a medium non-stick skillet place the ground beef, carrot, garlic and onion powder. Cook until beef is browned and carrot is tender. Drain.

Add the tomato sauce and ½ tsp. chili powder to skillet. Finely chop the kidney beans and add to meat mixture. Stir well and set aside.

Sprinkle bread lightly with chili powder. With a rolling pin, roll in both directions to form a square and flatten bread as thin as possible without tearing it. Spoon an equal amount of filling into the center of each square. Fold edges over to form triangles. Moisten edges of bread and press down with the tines of a fork to seal. Turn over and repeat on other side. At this point, you may freeze . . . or place on baking sheet and bake, uncovered, for 15 minutes or until toasted. Allow to cool and serve.

BUNDLES OF JOY!

This is a perfect special dish for Mommy or Daddy to share with baby. The recipe makes 1 adult serving and 1 child serving.

2   inch long julienned strips of fresh vegetables, about 10 each (carrot, zucchini and green beans)
⅓   cup plain yogurt
⅓   cup fine dry whole wheat bread crumbs
3   tbsp. shredded jack cheese
1   tbsp. fresh chopped parsley
1   tbsp. fresh chopped chives
2–3 sole fillets (approximately ½ lb.)

Preheat oven to 350°. Steam vegetables in a steamer basket until tender 5–7 minutes. While vegetables are steaming, in a small mixing bowl, stir together the yogurt, bread crumbs, cheese, parsley and chives.

With a rolling pin, slightly flatten the fish fillets. Spread the yogurt mixture down one side of each fillet. Lay the vegetables across the middle of the fillets with the ends sticking out. Roll out each fillet like a jelly roll.

Place in a greased shallow ovenproof dish with the seam sides down. Bake, covered for 20–30 minutes or until fish is no longer translucent.

Allow to cool and cut into slices like sushi.

4

Main Dishes

I have broken down this chapter into 3 categories (main dishes with meat, main dishes with fish and meatless main dishes) to make it easier for families on a vegetarian diet or someone scanning for a specific meal.

I recommend using sole fillets in the fish recipes. Sole is a boneless, mild fish that can be found in almost any grocery store. If sole is not available, I suggest cod. This is also a mild, versatile fish, but be sure to check for bones.

I have included items that are perfect for breakfast, lunch or dinner. I don't specify which because I believe that a baby's diet should be without such limits. Babies need variety and serving only pancakes for breakfast will soon produce only yawns. Go ahead and serve meatballs for breakfast and French toast with green beans for dinner. Your baby won't recognize this as a culinary faux pas, and she will certainly never develop a taste for boredom!

So, throw out your preconceived dining rules when feeding your baby or toddler. You may accidentally stumble onto some interesting snack ideas in addition to the main dishes.

MAIN DISHES WITH MEAT

SWEET-ISH MEATBALLS

These can be served with or without the sauce but the sweetness of the sauce is usually preferred by most babies.

$1/2$　lb. ground meat (beef, chicken, turkey, etc.)
$1/2$　cup very tender cooked long grain brown rice
$1/3$　cup fine dry whole wheat bread crumbs
1　small egg
1 · tbsp. milk, breast milk, or formula
2　tsp. snipped fresh parsley
$1/2$　tsp. onion powder
$1^{1}/_4$　cups water
　　yogurt sauce (recipe below)

Combine all ingredients, except water and yogurt sauce, thoroughly in a medium mixing bowl. Form into 1-inch balls. Pour water into a 10-inch non-stick skillet. Add meatballs. Bring to boil, then reduce heat. Cover and simmer, stirring often, for 15–20 minutes or until meatballs are cooked through. Drain water and follow directions for yogurt sauce below.

YOGURT SAUCE

$1/2$　cup plain yogurt
2　tbsp. apple juice concentrate
1　tbsp. whole wheat flour

Combine all ingredients in a medium saucepan. Heat over low flame until mixture boils and thickens. Continue cooking and stirring 1 minute longer.

Remove from heat. Add meatballs and toss. Cool to room temperature and serve. Separate into serving sizes before freezing.

FAUX SAUSAGE

You can use this recipe in dishes calling for sausage, such as lasagne. Just eliminate the bread crumbs. It's a much healthier alternative for the whole family!

¾ lb. ground lean pork, turkey or combination
½ cup fresh whole wheat bread crumbs
(approximately 1 small slice)
1 egg
2 tbsp. finely chopped parsley
1 tbsp. minced onion
1 clove garlic, minced or pressed
1 tsp. fennel seeds
½ tsp. chili powder
½ tsp. powdered thyme
¼ tsp. allspice
dash pepper

Mix all ingredients together in a medium mixing bowl. Form into 1-inch balls and press flat to make small patties. Cook patties over medium heat in a large non-stick skillet until cooked through, turning to brown both sides. Allow to cool and serve whole or cut in pieces. May be frozen.

BEEFY MAC

When the cheese cools, it causes all of the ingredients to "bind" together creating chunks for babies to easily grasp with their little fingers.

½	lb. lean ground beef
2	tbsp. minced onion
1	small clove garlic, crushed
4	oz. unsalted tomato sauce
½	cup mozzarella cheese
1	tbsp. grated Parmesan cheese
¼	tsp. dried oregano
⅛	tsp. cinnamon
	dash nutmeg
2	cups cooked whole wheat elbow macaroni (approximately 1 cup uncooked)

Preheat oven to 350°. Cook the ground beef, onion and garlic in a medium non-stick skillet until meat is browned. Drain. Stir in the tomato sauce, mozzarella and Parmesan cheeses, oregano, cinnamon and nutmeg. Stir until cheese is melted. Add the macaroni and toss gently until well combined. Pour mixture into an ungreased 1 quart casserole dish. Cook, covered, for 30–35 minutes or until heated through. Cool and serve at room temperature. May be frozen.

HERBED LIVER

Liver is a great meat for babies. Not only is it high in iron, but it is tender enough for even toothless babies to eat!

½	lb. beef liver
¼–½	cup whole wheat flour
2	tsp. margarine or olive oil
¼	tsp. chopped fresh parsley
¼	tsp. dried thyme
⅛	tsp. dried sage
⅛	tsp. dried rosemary

Wash liver and pat dry with a paper towel. Cut liver across the grain into ½-inch wide strips. Coat with flour; shaking off excess.

Heat margarine or oil in a small skillet. Sauté liver until slightly browned on both sides 1–2 minutes. Add the herbs and sauté 2–3 minutes longer. Allow to cool and serve strips whole or for babies without molars, cut into tiny bite size pieces. May be frozen.

BABY HAD A LITTLE LAMB

Meatballs in sauce are a great finger food for toddlers. For that Greek flavor, I used lamb in these but they work just as well with a more traditional ground beef or poultry.

1/2   lb. lean ground lamb
1/2   tsp. cumin
1/2   tsp. coriander
1/4   tsp. nutmeg
1/4   tsp. turmeric
1/8   tsp. cinnamon
1/4   cup low or no sodium chicken broth*
1   clove garlic, minced or pressed
1   tsp. MRS. DASH or other salt-free seasoning
1/4   cup plain yogurt

Preheat broiler. In a medium mixing bowl combine the lamb, cumin, coriander, turmeric, nutmeg and cinnamon. Form into 1-inch balls. Place on a broiler rack and broil 6 inches from heat, turning often. Cook until meatballs are browned but still moist.

In large skillet, combine the broth, garlic and salt-free seasoning. Bring to a boil. Add meatballs, lower heat and simmer until broth is absorbed 10–15 minutes. Remove from heat and add yogurt. Stir gently to coat. Allow to cool and serve whole or cut in half. Separate into serving size portions before freezing.

*Read label to be sure that broth has no MSG in it. Health Valley makes a great no sodium/no MSG brand. Look for it in the soup or diet section of the grocery store.

ORANGE YOU A YUMMY SALAD!*

If you can't find mandarin oranges in their own juice, use a can in light syrup, then thoroughly drain and rinse the oranges in water before using.

½   cup tender cooked turkey or chicken cut into
     ¼ inch cubes
½   can mandarin oranges in own juice
1   tbsp. mayonnaise

Drain the oranges, reserving the juice. Stir together 1 tbsp. of the juice and the mayonnaise. In a small mixing bowl combine the turkey or chicken and the oranges. Add the mayonnaise mixture, toss and serve.

*This should only be given to toddlers with molars.

LIVER GONE NUTS!

It is fairly common for toddlers to become anemic. Eating liver can help prevent this iron deficiency, and believe it or not, babies usually like it!

½   lb. chicken livers
1   tsp. olive oil
2   tsp. minced onion
1   small clove garlic, minced or pressed
¼   cup low or no sodium chicken broth*
2   tbsp. ground pecans**
¼   tsp. lemon rind
     dash pepper

Wash livers and pat dry with a paper towel. Remove any extraneous fat, fibers or discolorations. Cut larger pieces into halves or quarters.

Heat oil in a small non-stick skillet over medium-low heat. Add the onions and garlic and sauté until limp. Add the livers. Sauté until liver are no longer pink. Drain. Stir in broth, pecans, lemon rind and pepper. Cook over low heat 10 minutes or until liquid is absorbed and meat is browned, stirring frequently. May be frozen.

*Read labels to be sure there is no MSG in the broth. Health Valley makes a great no sodium/no MSG brand. Look for it in the soup or diet sections of the grocery store.
**A food processor is recommended for this.

LES ENFANTS PATÉ

You can cut this paté into cubes or spread it on whole wheat bread to make a sandwich. To be appreciated only by the truly sophisticated juvenile gourmets!

1	tsp. margarine
1/2	lb. chicken livers, washed and patted dry
1	tbsp. finely chopped onion
2	tbsp. cream cheese
1	tsp. lemon juice
1	tsp. margarine
1/8	tsp. dry mustard
	dash pepper

In a medium non-stick skillet over medium-low heat, melt the first tsp. margarine. Add the livers and onion. Cook 7–10 minutes and stir until liver is no longer pink in middle. Transfer liver mixture and drippings to a food processor or blender. Add remaining ingredients and process until smooth.

Spread into a greased mini loaf pan, cover and chill for 6 hours or overnight. Remove from pan and slice.

THIS LITTLE PIGGY . . .

There is a little taste of Hawaii in every meatball! This recipe is great for using up those last jars of baby food sitting on your shelf.

4	jars ham baby food
½	cup fine dry bread crumbs
1	small egg, beaten
1	tsp. onion powder
½	tsp. dry mustard
2	tsp. margarine
¼	cup pineapple juice concentrate
¼	cup water
2	tsp. vinegar
2	tsp. cornstarch
¼	tsp. dry mustard

In a medium mixing bowl place the ham, bread crumbs, egg, onion powder, and mustard. Mix well. Roll mixture into ½-inch balls.

In a large non-stick skillet, melt the margarine over medium heat. Add the meatballs and gently stir until well browned on all sides. Remove meatballs to a platter.

In a small bowl, combine the pineapple juice concentrate, water, vinegar, cornstarch and mustard. Pour into the skillet. Heat over low heat until bubbly.

Return meatballs to the skillet. Cook, stirring occasionally, 5 minutes more. Allow to cool and serve meatballs whole or cut in half. May be frozen.

CHICKEN LIVERS WITH PASTA

You may crinkle your nose at the thought of eating liver, but don't deny your baby this near perfect food. Added benefits? Babies usually like the taste, and it's very inexpensive!

½	lb. chicken livers, cut up
1	tbsp. vegetable oil
2	tbsp. finely chopped onion
1	small clove garlic, minced
½	of a 15-ounce can salt-free tomato sauce
1	tsp. Italian seasoning
1	cup whole wheat or enriched pasta in an "easy to grasp" shape, cooked until tender
	Parmesan cheese (optional)

In a small skillet, cook the liver in hot oil over medium heat for about 5 minutes or until slightly pink in the center. Remove from the skillet. Add the onions and garlic to skillet and cook until tender. Stir in the tomato sauce and Italian seasoning. Cover and simmer for 10 minutes. Stir in the chicken livers and simmer uncovered for a few minutes or until heated through. Pour over pasta and sprinkle with Parmesan cheese, if desired.

MAIN DISHES WITH FISH

STUFFED TUNA SANDWICH

The traditional tuna salad sandwich has gotten even healthier by "stuffing" some veggies into it!

3   oz. low sodium tuna in water,
     drained and flaked*
1   hard cooked egg
½   small carrot, finely grated
½   small zucchini, finely grated
2   tbsp. mayonnaise
     whole wheat bread

Mix together the first 5 ingredients. Spread between 2–4 slices of whole wheat bread. Cut into quarters to serve.

*This is usually located in the diet aisle of the grocery store.

TUNA FINGERS

My baby will eat this whole protein-laden batch in one sitting!

3   oz. low sodium tuna in water,
     drained and flaked*
3   oz. cream cheese
1   tbsp. snipped fresh parsley
1   tsp. lemon juice
1   tsp. low sodium soy sauce

In a small mixing bowl, combine all ingredients with a fork. Form into 2-inch "fingers" and serve.

*This is usually located in the diet aisle of the grocery store.

LEMONY TUNA SQUARES

For toddlers who don't like the strong taste of tuna, this is the perfect recipe. The lemon juice and cheese mask the powerful flavor of the fish.

1	slice whole wheat bread, torn into small pieces
1/2	cup shredded cheddar cheese
3	oz. low sodium tuna in water, drained and flaked*
1/3	cup milk, breast milk or formula
1	egg yolk
1	tsp. lemon juice
1/4	tsp. onion powder
1/4	tsp. poppy seeds
1/8	tsp. dry mustard
2	egg whites

Preheat oven to 350°. In a medium mixing bowl combine the bread pieces, cheese, tuna, milk, egg yolk, lemon juice, onion powder, poppy seeds and dry mustard. Set aside.

Beat the egg whites until stiff. Fold into tuna mixture. Spread into a greased 1 quart square or rectangular casserole dish. Bake, uncovered, 30 minutes or until set. Allow to cool and cut into squares. May be frozen.

*This is usually located in the diet aisle of the grocery store.

COD CAKES

Turning your baby into a fish lover is easy—and so good for her!

1	cup cooked cod or other mild boneless fish
1/3	cup whole wheat bread crumbs
1/4	cup dry nonfat milk
1	tbsp. mayonnaise
2	tsp. snipped fresh parsley
1	tsp. chopped fresh chives
1/2	tsp. onion powder
1/4	tsp. minced garlic
1/3	cup water (approximately)

Finely crumble fish with fork in a medium mixing bowl. Add bread crumbs, mayonnaise, dry milk, parsley, chives, onion powder and garlic. Mix well. Add water, using more if mixture is not moist enough. Form into four 1-inch thick patties. Fry on both sides in preheated non-stick skillet over low heat until browned. May be frozen.

CRUSTY FISH

This is a dish the whole family will love!

3/4	lb. mild boneless fish fillets
1	tbsp. margarine, melted
	dash pepper
1	green onion, finely chopped
1/4	cup grated cheddar cheese
3	tbsp. grated Parmesan cheese
2	tbsp. fine fresh whole wheat bread crumbs
1	tsp. MRS. DASH or other salt-free seasoning

Preheat oven to 425°. Arrange fillets in a greased, shallow baking dish in a single layer. Brush with the margarine. Sprinkle with the pepper and green onion.

In a small mixing bowl combine the cheddar and Parmesan cheeses, bread crumbs and salt-free seasoning. Sprinkle over the fillets. Bake, uncovered, 20–25 minutes or until fish flakes easily and the cheese is melted. Allow to cool and cut into serving size pieces. May be frozen.

JELLY FISH

Who says you can't put jelly on fish? Your baby will like it so much that she'll never guess you're "breaking the rules"!

¼   lb. fish fillet or fillets
1   tsp. margarine, melted
1   tbsp. 100% fruit jelly

Preheat oven to 350°. Lay out fish fillets in a shallow, greased baking dish in a single layer. Brush with margarine and cover. Bake in oven for 10–20 minutes (depending on thickness) until fish flakes easily. Remove fish from oven and uncover. Preheat broiler. Gently spread the jelly over the fillets. Place under broiler for 3 minutes or until the top is glazed and brown. Allow to cool and serve. May be frozen.

PIZZA FISH

What child doesn't like the taste of pizza? Even non-fish eaters will be pleasantly surprised when they taste the pizza more than the fish!

½   lb. mild boneless fish fillets
¼   cup salt- and sugar-free spaghetti sauce
¼   cup shredded mozzarella

Preheat oven to 350°. Arrange fish fillets on a well-greased baking sheet in a single layer. Pour spaghetti sauce over fillets. Bake uncovered 15–20 minutes or until fish flakes easily with a fork. Sprinkle with cheese and return to oven until cheese melts, about 5 minutes. Allow to cool and cut into serving size pieces. May be frozen.

FISH STIX

This whole wheat breading is much better for your baby than the white version you buy in the store—and minus the salt!

½   lb. mild boneless fish fillets
1   egg
1   tbsp. milk, breast milk or formula
½   cup fine dry whole wheat bread crumbs
½   tsp. onion powder
2   tsp. vegetable oil

Pat fish dry. Cut into 1-inch strips. In a small mixing bowl, beat together the egg and milk. In another small bowl mix the bread crumbs and onion powder.

Heat the oil in a large non-stick skillet over medium heat. Dip the fish strips in the egg mixture and then in the bread crumbs. Place in skillet and cook 3 minutes per side or until cooked through and browned. Allow to cool and serve. May be frozen.

SCALLOP BITES

One cup for Mommy or Daddy and one cup for baby! What a special treat!

1	cup water
1	tsp. vinegar
1	bay leaf
	dash crumbled tarragon
4	oz. scallops, halved if using large scallops
1	tbsp. fine dry whole wheat bread crumbs
1	tbsp. grated Parmesan cheese
1	tbsp. plain yogurt
2	tsp. mayonnaise
1/8	tsp. garlic powder
	dash pepper

In a medium saucepan, bring the water, vinegar, bay leaf and tarragon to a boil. Add scallops and lower heat. Simmer 2 minutes or until no longer translucent. Drain liquid; reserving scallops. Arrange in 2 small custard-sized Pyrex baking dishes. Set aside.

In a small bowl combine the bread crumbs, Parmesan cheese, yogurt, mayonnaise, garlic powder and pepper. Spoon over the scallops and toss gently to coat.

Broil for 5 minutes or until slightly browned. Allow to cool and serve. May be frozen.

GEFILTE FISH FRY

Growing up in my Jewish household, gefilte fish was always a staple! Of course, back then, I didn't realize it was good for me too!

1	12 oz. jar low sodium gefilte fish*
1	small carrot, shredded
1	tbsp. chopped onion
1/4	cup matzo meal
1	egg
1	tsp. lemon juice
1	tsp. dijon mustard
1/2	tsp. dry dill
1/2	tsp. garlic powder
1	tsp. vegetable oil

Drain fish. In a blender or food processor, process the fish, carrot and onion. Add the matzo meal, egg, lemon juice, mustard, dill and garlic powder. Process lightly for a few seconds. Allow to stand about 10 minutes.

Heat oil in a large non-stick skillet over medium heat. Drop fish batter by tablespoons onto hot skillet without touching each other. Cook on both sides until browned, flattening slightly with spatula. Allow to cool and serve whole or cut into pieces. May be frozen.

*You can find gefilte fish in the kosher section of the international food aisle at most grocery stores.

LIVER STIX

This is a "child friendly" way to get them to eat liver.

½ lb. liver, cut into ½-inch strips
3 tbsp. whole wheat bread crumbs
2 tbsp. nonfat dry milk
1 tbsp. Parmesan cheese
¼ tsp. garlic powder
¼ tsp. onion powder
2 tsp. margarine

In a sealable bag place the bread crumbs, dry milk, Parmesan cheese, garlic powder and onion powder. Shake to combine. Add the liver sticks and shake to coat. Melt margarine in a small skillet over medium heat. Add liver to skillet and fry on both sides until browned and cooked through, about 3–5 minutes.

BAKED SCALLOPS

Scallops come naturally in the perfect finger food shape!

½ lb. scallops
¼ cup whole wheat bread crumbs
1 tsp. Italian seasoning
¼ cup milk
  vegetable spray
  paprika

Preheat oven to 450°. Rinse scallops and pat dry. In small bowl mix together the bread crumbs and Italian seasoning. Set aside. Dip scallops in milk and then roll in the bread crumbs. Place in a single layer on sprayed baking pan. Sprinkle with paprika. Bake 10–15 minutes depending on size and thickness.

FISHY LOAVES

For this recipe you can used flaked and cooked fresh fish or canned tuna or salmon.*

1	cup flaked fish
⅓	cup canned low sodium tomatoes, chopped
¾	cup fresh, soft whole wheat bread crumbs
1	egg
2	tbsp. minced onion
⅛	tsp. dried sage
	vegetable oil

Preheat oven to 350°. Mix together all ingredients. Press into 2–3 (depending on size) mini loaf pans that have been lightly oiled. Bake 30 minutes or until firm. Allow to cool and slice. May be frozen.

*You can usually find low sodium tuna and salmon in the diet section of the grocery store. May be frozen.

CORNY FISH

The cornmeal gives this a distinct taste that children usually love.

¼	cup cornmeal
¼	tsp. marjoram
1	tbsp. safflower oil
½	lb. boneless fish fillets

Preheat oven to 400°. In a small, wide, shallow bowl, combine the cornmeal and marjoram. Gently press fish into the mixture to coat both sides. Rub a shallow baking pan with ½ of the oil. Arrange fish in a single layer. Drizzle with remaining oil. Bake 15–25 minutes depending on thickness of fish.

MEATLESS MAIN DISHES

BABY ALFREDO

A healthful but still creamy version of the original that you might just want to try yourself!

½	cup uncooked whole wheat pasta spirals or other easy to grasp whole wheat pasta
¼	cup ricotta cheese
¼	cup unsalted frozen petite peas, defrosted and drained
2	tbsp. milk, breast milk or formula
1	tbsp. grated Parmesan cheese
2	tsp. snipped parsley
⅛	tsp. nutmeg

Cook pasta according to package directions until very tender. Meanwhile, stir together, in a medium mixing bowl, the remaining ingredients. Drain pasta and add to cheese mixture. Toss gently and serve.

PASTA BAKE

Pasta is great but adding cheese gives it that extra little protein and calcium boost.

¾ cup uncooked whole wheat pasta
  (spirals, shells, rigatoni, etc.)
¼ cup salt- and sugar-free spaghetti sauce
3 tbsp. mozzarella cheese

Cook pasta according to package directions until very soft. Drain. In a small individual casserole dish (or individual souffle dish) mix together the pasta, spaghetti sauce, and mozzarella cheese. Bake in a 350° oven for 30 minutes or until cheese is melted. Allow to cool and serve in pieces. May be frozen.

MACARONI AND CHEESE PUFF

Just like a French souffle but a lot more fun!

1 egg white
⅛ tsp. cream of tartar
¼ cup milk, breast milk or formula
1 slice American cheese
1 egg yolk, beaten
¼ cup whole wheat macaroni, cooked according
  to package directions until very soft
½ slice whole wheat bread, crumbled
1 tsp. chopped green onion

Preheat oven to 325°. Beat egg whites and cream of tartar until stiff. Set aside.

Heat milk and cheese over low heat until cheese has melted. Remove from heat and add egg yolk. Stir well. Add macaroni, bread crumbs and onion. Stir until crumbs are soft. Fold in egg whites.

Pour into a small, greased individual casserole or souffle dish and bake 45 minutes or until knife inserted in center comes out clean. Allow to cool and break into pieces. May be frozen.

PETER RABBIT PASTA

4	oz. uncooked whole wheat corkscrew pasta or any pasta easy to grasp with the fingers
1	tsp. olive oil
1	tbsp. finely chopped onion
1	small clove garlic, minced or pressed
1	small carrot, shredded
1	small zucchini, shredded
1	small tomato, peeled and chopped fine
1/2	cup mozzarella cheese
2	tbsp. grated Parmesan cheese

Cook pasta according to package directions until very tender. Drain and set aside.

Heat oil in a medium non-stick skillet over medium heat. Add onion and garlic and cook until limp. Add carrot, zucchini, and tomato. Cook and stir 5 minutes longer. Remove from heat.

Stir in the mozzarella, 1 tbsp. Parmesan cheese and pasta. Turn into a greased 1 quart casserole dish. Sprinkle with remaining Parmesan. Bake 15 minutes or until cheese melts. Allow to cool and break into pieces. May be frozen.

BROC-A-NOODLE-DOO PIES!

Broccoli has never tasted this good!

6   oz. whole wheat macaroni, cooked according to
    package directions until very tender
1   egg yolk
2   tsp. finely chopped fresh chives
2   eggs
1   egg white
½   cup creamed cottage cheese or ricotta cheese
½   tsp. chopped fresh chives
5   oz. frozen chopped broccoli,
    defrosted and drained well
½   cup cheddar cheese, shredded
    paprika

Preheat oven to 375°. Place the macaroni, egg yolk and chives in a food processor or blender. Grind until almost smooth. With wet fingers, press mixture along the bottom and sides of a greased 6 cup muffin tin. Bake 10 minutes, remove from oven and allow to cool.

Increase oven temperature to 425°. In a medium bowl, beat the eggs, egg white, cottage cheese and chives together. Add the broccoli and cheddar. Stir well. Pour evenly into each muffin tin. Sprinkle lightly with paprika. Bake, uncovered, 15 minutes. Reduce oven temperature to 300° and bake an additional 15–20 minutes or until knife inserted in center comes out clean. Allow to cool and serve whole or in quarters. May be frozen.

GEORGIE PORGIE SPINACH PIES

These are so cute and delicious, you can use them as hors d'oeuvres at your next party!

1/4 cup chopped mushrooms
1 tsp. margarine
2 eggs
1/2 cup plain yogurt
1/2 cup small curd cottage cheese
1/4 cup grated Parmesan cheese
2 tbsp. whole wheat flour
1/2 tsp. onion powder
3/4 cup jack cheese, shredded
5 oz. box frozen chopped spinach,
thawed and squeezed dry

Preheat oven to 350°. Sauté the mushrooms in margarine in a small non-stick skillet until limp. Set aside.

In a blender or food processor, blend the eggs, yogurt, cottage cheese, Parmesan cheese, flour and onion powder. Pour into a mixing bowl. Fold in the mushrooms, jack cheese and spinach. Pour into a greased, 12-cup muffin tin about 1/2 full. Bake for 25–30 minutes or until knife inserted in centers comes out clean. Allow to cool and serve whole or in quarters. May be frozen.

SUNNY SQUARES

You'll have to make these to find out why I gave them this title!

5	oz. frozen chopped spinach
1	tbsp. olive oil
½	tsp. turmeric
1	tbsp. minced onion
1	small green onion, finely chopped
4	oz. firm tofu
1	tsp. MRS. DASH or other salt-free seasoning
1	cup cooked brown rice
	(approximately ½ cup uncooked)

Preheat oven to 325°. Defrost spinach and reserve 1 tbsp. of the liquid.

Heat ½ of the olive oil in a small non-stick skillet over medium-high heat. Add the turmeric and both onions and sauté until soft. Remove from heat.

In a blender or food processor, beat together the tofu, salt-free seasoning, remaining oil and juice from spinach. Transfer to a medium mixing bowl. Add the spinach, onions and the rice. Spread into a greased 1 quart square or rectangular casserole dish. Bake for 30 minutes or until set. Allow to cool and cut into squares. May be frozen.

CONFETTI SQUARES

Babies can't help being attracted to this colorful food!

1½ cups shredded carrots
¾ cup frozen defrosted green beans or
   fresh green beans that have been steamed
   until very tender, finely chopped
¾ cup water
⅓ cup long grain brown rice
¾ cup shredded or torn American cheese
¼ cup milk, breast milk, or formula
1 beaten egg
1 tbsp. minced dried onion

Preheat oven to 350°. In a medium saucepan combine carrots, green beans, water and rice. Bring to a boil, then reduce heat. Cover and simmer, stirring occasionally about 20 minutes or until rice is very tender. Uncover and add cheese. Stir until cheese melts. Remove from heat and stir in milk, eggs and onion. Pour a 1¼–2 quart square or rectangular casserole dish. Bake for 25–30 minutes or until set. Allow to cool and cut into squares. May be frozen.

NUTTY LOAVES

Nuts are usually a no-no in baby fare because of the choking hazard they pose, but they are so healthful that it's a shame to leave them out completely. These loaves are a great way to keep those nuts in your baby's diet.

1	cup cooked brown rice (approximately ½ cup uncooked)
½	cup rolled oats
½	cup shredded cheddar cheese
½	cup shredded carrot
¼	cup dry whole wheat bread crumbs
2	eggs, lightly beaten
2	tbsp. ground walnuts*
2	tbsp. ground, unsalted sunflower seeds*
2	tbsp. sesame seeds
1	tbsp. minced onion
1	tsp. MRS. DASH or other salt-free seasoning dash pepper

Preheat oven and cookie sheet to 350°. Combine all of the ingredients in a medium mixing bowl. Pack into 2–3 (depending on size) greased mini loaf pans. Bake for 30–35 minutes or until firm. Allow to cool, unmold and slice or cut in cubes to serve. May be frozen.

*I suggest grinding the nuts and unsalted sunflower seeds together in a food processor or blender.

GREEN EGGS AND ...

"Sam-I-Am" highly recommends this one!

1   egg
2   tbsp. milk, breast milk, or formula
2   tbsp. chopped frozen spinach,
       defrosted and squeezed dry
2   tbsp. grated cheese (cheddar, American, etc.)

Beat all ingredients with wire whisk. Cook over low heat in a small non-stick skillet, stirring constantly, until egg is well done. Remove from pan and cool before serving.

TODDLER TOFU STRIPS

Tofu is a great protein food with a perfect texture that babies can eat without chewing.

1   egg
4   oz. firm tofu
¼   cup fine dry whole wheat bread crumbs
1   tbsp. grated Parmesan cheese
1   tsp. garlic powder
1   tsp. dried parsley

Preheat oven to 350°. Beat egg in a small bowl and set aside. Cut tofu into 2 inch strips, about 1 inch thick. Combine the bread crumbs, Parmesan cheese, garlic powder and parsley in a small, shallow bowl. Gently dip tofu in the egg, then roll in crumb mixture. Place on a greased cookie sheet and bake for 15 minutes. Allow to cool on pan before removing. May be frozen.

CASA DIA*

Quesadillas are a great traveling food and are much better than a sandwich because they can't pull the bread apart!

2   corn tortillas or
      small whole wheat flour tortillas
1/4 cup shredded jack cheese
2   tsp. diced mild green chilies

Sprinkle cheese and chilies over one tortilla and cover with the other. Cook on a microwave-safe plate in microwave for 30 seconds to 1 minute or until cheese is melted. Allow to cool and cut into quarters to serve.

*For toddlers with molars.

FRENCH TOAST SANDWICH

This tastes like a cheesecake sandwich—try it for brunch.

2   slices whole wheat bread
1   egg
1   tbsp. milk, breast milk or formula
1–2 tbsp. light cream cheese
2   tsp. 100% fruit jelly (optional)

Beat the egg and milk together in a wide shallow bowl. Spread cream cheese over one slice of bread and, if using the jelly, spread that on the other slice. Bring the slices together to make a "cream cheese sandwich." Soak sandwich on both sides in egg mixture until all liquid is absorbed. Fry over low heat in a non-stick skillet on both sides until browned. Allow to cool and cut into quarters to serve. May be frozen.

PEANUT BUTTER AND JELLY TOAST

A big glass of milk complements this sandwich perfectly!

1   tbsp. sugar- and salt-free peanut butter
1–3   tbsp. milk, breast milk or formula
2   slices whole wheat bread
1   egg
3   tbsp. unsweetened grape juice concentrate

Mix peanut butter and milk together in a small bowl until smooth and thinned out. Spread peanut mixture on both slices of bread and put together to make a sandwich. Beat egg and grape juice together in a small shallow bowl. Soak sandwich on both sides in egg mixture until most or all of the mixture is absorbed. Fry in a non-stick skillet over low heat on both sides until browned. May be frozen.

SWEETEST FRENCH TOAST

No sugar at all, yet this recipe will satisfy any sweet tooth!

2–3   tbsp. milk, breast milk or formula
1½   tbsp. sugar- and salt-free peanut butter
1½   tbsp. finely chopped raisins
1   tsp. 100% fruit spread
½   tsp. cinnamon
2   slices whole wheat bread
1   egg
2   tbsp. milk, breast milk or formula

Combine 2 tablespoons milk, peanut butter, raisins, fruit spread and cinnamon. Mix until well combined and peanut butter is thinned, using additional milk if necessary. Spread mixture on 1 slice of bread and top with the remaining slice to make a sandwich.

Beat together the egg and remaining 2 tbsp. of milk. Dip the sandwich on both sides into egg mixture. Fry in a non-stick skillet over low heat on both sides until browned. Allow to cool and cut into quarters to serve. May be frozen.

5

Vegetables

We all know that vegetables are important in our diets, yet most of us don't eat our daily recommendation (5 servings of vegetables and fruits). Vegetables are just as important to babies and children, (Popeye wasn't half wrong about the spinach thing!) and they will usually be one of a baby's first foods. Most babies will eat the pureed variety with gusto; but when a baby reaches the finger food stage, and a variety of other goodies are being offered, vegetables usually end up taking a back seat (if any seat at all!). For most children, the extent of their vegetable consumption ends up being French fries!

When serving vegetables to babies and toddlers, you also have to consider the many choking hazards associated with raw vegetables (carrot, celery, zucchini, etc.). Since you have to cook them, why not do it creatively! I'm sure your baby would much rather eat "3-B Burgers" than a lump of broccoli and brussels sprouts.

That is what this chapter is all about—preparing and serving vegetables in a creative manner so that your child never sticks out her tongue when you mention the words "zucchini" and "lunch" in the same sentence!

Don't immediately start off with the recipes that contain your child's favorite vegetable. Instead, if she has an aversion to spinach, but you know she needs to eat more green leafy vegetables, start with a spinach dish. You might be surprised when your baby eats the spinach because it is combined with other ingredients. If she does, you have an invaluable addition to her diet.

Vegetables should definitely be offered in their natural state to begin with; but if your baby, like scores of other children, refuses to part his lips for peas and carrots, then simply refer to this chapter for some ideas. Hopefully, those lips won't be shut for long!

SMALL FRIES

I prefer to use white rose potatoes because the skin is high in fiber and unlike russet potatoes it is thin and not a choking hazard to babies. Of course, you can use russets; just peel them first.

1   large white rose potato, washed and scrubbed
1   egg white
2   tbsp. water
¼   cup wheat germ
½   tsp. dried rosemary leaves, crushed
½   tsp. garlic powder
    cooking spray

Preheat oven to 400°. Lightly spray cookie sheet with cooking spray. Cut potato lengthwise into 16 pieces about ¼ inch thick.

Beat the water and egg white in a small bowl until frothy. Combine wheat germ, rosemary leaves and garlic powder in another small bowl.

Dip potatoes into egg mixture and then into wheat germ mixture. Place slices on cookie sheet without touching each other. Bake 25–30 minutes or until potatoes are browned and tender.

HASH BROWN TATERS

This is a great way to use leftover baked potatoes from dinner.

1   baked potato
1   tsp. margarine
     dash garlic powder
     dash chili powder

Cut potato into ½ inch cubes and remove skin for younger babies. Heat the margarine in a small skillet. Add potatoes. Sprinkle with garlic powder and chili powder. Cook until slightly brown. Allow to cool and serve.

POTATOES IN A BLANKET

Unless your baby is older and knows that the foil isn't edible, I'd remove it and serve the potatoes on a plate.

1   large unpeeled white rose potato,
     cut into ½-inch cubes
1   tbsp. whole wheat flour
2   tsp. grated Parmesan cheese
¼   cup shredded cheddar cheese
1   tsp. margarine

Preheat oven to 375°. Combine potato cubes, flour and Parmesan cheese. Stir to coat.

Cut one 12-inch square of aluminum foil and a

matching square of waxed paper. Place the waxed paper on top of foil. Place potato mixture on center of waxed paper. Sprinkle with cheddar cheese and dot with margarine. Bring up corners of foil and seal. Bake for 40–45 minutes or until tender. Open foil, allow to cool and serve. May be frozen.

SPUDUMPLINGS

These can also be used in soups.

2   medium potatoes, peeled, boiled until
        tender and mashed
1.   egg lightly beaten
1½ tsp. MRS. DASH or other
        herbal salt-free seasoning
¼–½   cup fine dry whole wheat bread crumbs

Bring a large pot of water to a boil. Meanwhile, in a medium mixing bowl, combine the mashed potatoes, egg, seasonings and enough bread crumbs so potatoes can be formed into balls. Form into 1-inch balls. Drop into boiling water. Reduce heat and simmer 5–7 minutes. Remove with a slotted spoon. Cool and serve. Divide into serving sizes before freezing.

STUFFED SPUDUMPLINGS

After forming potato in balls, punch a hole in center and fill with cooked ground beef, chicken or pork. Close hole and re-form into balls. Cook as directed.

SWEET SPUDUMPLINGS

1   small sweet potato or yam, boiled until tender,
    peeled and mashed
1   small ripe banana mashed
1   egg
2   tbsp. orange juice
½   cup wheat germ
¼–½ cup fine dry whole wheat bread crumbs

Bring a large pot of water to a boil. Meanwhile, in
a medium mixing bowl, combine the mashed sweet
potato, banana, egg, orange juice, wheat germ and
enough crumbs so mixture can be rolled into balls.
Roll into 1-inch balls. Drop into boiling water,
reduce heat and simmer for 5–9 minutes or until
balls have risen to the top. Remove with a slotted
spoon. Cool and serve. Separate into serving sized
portions before freezing.

HOME SWEET HOME FRIES

1   small sweet potato or yam, peeled and
    cut lengthwise into ½-inch thick sticks
1   tbsp. apple juice concentrate
2   tsp. margarine, melted

Line a broiler pan with aluminum foil and preheat broiler. Boil the potatoes in a covered pot of
water for 5–7 minutes or until crisp-tender. Drain.
Combine the apple juice concentrate and margarine in a medium mixing bowl. Add the potatoes
and toss gently to coat. Arrange on broiler pan in a
single layer. Broil 3 minutes per side or until lightly
browned. Allow to cool and serve. May be frozen.

CANDIED APPLE YAMS

Apples and yams were always my daughter's favorite foods. I knew that by combining them for this dish, I couldn't miss! She loved it!

1	small yam, peeled and diced into 1/2-inch cubes
1/2	medium sized apple, peeled, cored and diced into 1/2-inch cubes
1/3	cup apple juice concentrate
1	tbsp. orange juice concentrate
1/4	tsp. ground cinnamon
	dash nutmeg
2	tsp. corn starch

Preheat oven to 350°. Boil yam in a small covered saucepan filled with water 5–7 minutes or until crisp-tender. Drain and set aside.

Combine both juices, cinnamon and nutmeg in a medium saucepan. Stir in the cornstarch. Cook over low heat until bubbly. Remove from heat and add yams and apples. Stir to coat. Transfer to a 1-quart buttered baking dish. Bake, covered, for 30 minutes or until potato and apple are tender. Cool and serve. May be frozen.

CARROT FINGERS

I made these into finger shapes for simplicity but you can shape them any way you want—maybe into a pretzel or heart shape!

¹/₂	cup cold mashed potatoes
1	small carrot, *finely* grated
1	small shallot, *finely* grated
1	egg
¹/₄	cup *finely* grated jack cheese
¹/₈	tsp. nutmeg
¹/₈	tsp. ground allspice
	dash white pepper
¹/₂–³/₄	cups whole wheat flour
1	tbsp. margarine, melted
1	tbsp. grated Parmesan cheese

Preheat oven to 325°. In a medium mixing bowl combine the potatoes with all except the last 3 ingredients. Starting with ¹/₂ cup flour, work in until a soft dough is formed, adding more as needed.

Bring a large pot of water to a boil. Roll dough into long ropes about ¹/₂ inch thick and cut into 2-inch pieces. Cook pieces in the boiling water until they rise to the surface. Remove with a slotted spoon. Place on a greased cookie sheet, brush with margarine and sprinkle with Parmesan cheese. Bake for 15–20 minutes or until lightly browned. Cool and serve. May be frozen.

CANDIED SQUASH

With only 2 ingredients, this is really simple to prepare and makes a great side dish.

2   small yellow crook neck squash
2   tbsp. apple juice concentrate

Slice squash into 1 inch rounds, then slice rounds into quarters. In small saucepan combine squash and apple juice concentrate. Bring to a boil. Cover and simmer for 15 minutes or until squash is very tender and liquid is absorbed. May be frozen.

RUGRAT-ATOUILLE

This is one of the messier finger foods, but babies love the sweet taste so it's worth it!

1   cup diced unpeeled zucchini
1   cup diced peeled eggplant
3   tbsp. unsalted tomato paste
3   tbsp. apple juice concentrate
1/8 tsp. dried basil

Steam the zucchini in a steamer basket 5 minutes or until crisp-tender. Add the eggplant and steam for 5 minutes more or until both vegetables are tender. Transfer the vegetables to a medium saucepan. Add the tomato paste, apple juice concentrate and basil. Gently stir over high heat until boiling. Lower heat, cover and simmer for 15 minutes or until liquid is absorbed, stirring occasionally. Cool to room temperature and serve. May be frozen.

CURDS AND WHEY CASSEROLE

Little Miss Muffett never had it so healthy!

1/2	lb. zucchini (approximately 1 small), shredded
1/4	cup chopped mushrooms
1	tbsp. finely chopped onion
1	tsp. vegetable oil
4	oz. cottage cheese
1/2	cup shredded cheddar cheese
1	egg, beaten
2	tsp. whole wheat flour
1	tsp. Italian seasoning
1/2	tsp. garlic powder

Preheat oven to 350°. Cook zucchini, mushrooms and onion in oil in a medium skillet over medium-high heat for 5 minutes or until vegetables are soft. Remove from heat and set aside.

Mix remaining ingredients in a medium mixing bowl. Stir in the vegetables. Pour into a greased 1/2–1 quart square or rectangular casserole dish. Bake 30–35 minutes or until knife inserted in center comes out clean. Allow to cool and cut into squares. May be frozen.

EGGPLANT PARMESAN

Serve with some tender buttered-pasta and you have a full meal.

4	slices unpeeled eggplant (cut horizontally from the middle), about 1 inch thick
2	tbsp. cottage cheese
1½	tbsp. unsalted tomato paste
2	tsp. water
2	tsp. plain yogurt
1	tsp. snipped parsley
⅛	tsp. garlic powder
⅛	tsp. oregano
1	tbsp. grated mozzarella cheese
2	tsp. grated Parmesan cheese

Preheat oven to 350°. In an uncovered medium skillet, simmer eggplant in 1 inch of water until very tender. Drain on a paper towel and pat dry. Gently peel off skin. Place eggplant in a small, shallow baking dish.

Blend together, in a small mixing bowl, the cottage cheese, tomato paste, water, yogurt, parsley, garlic powder and oregano. Spread over the eggplant. Sprinkle with the mozzarella and Parmesan. Bake, uncovered, for 30 minutes or until top is browned. Allow to cool completely and remove with a spatula. May be frozen.

3-B BURGERS

Broccoli, Brussels Sprouts and Bread Crumbs!

1/2	cup cooked broccoli*
1/2	cup cooked brussels sprouts*
1/2	cup milk, breast milk, or formula
1/4	cup cottage cheese
1	small egg
2	tsp. orange juice concentrate
1	tsp. snipped parsley
1/4	tsp. garlic powder
1/4	cup fine dry whole wheat bread crumbs

In a blender or food processor, combine the broccoli, brussels sprouts, milk, cottage cheese, egg, orange juice concentrate, parsley and garlic powder. Blend until smooth. Combine with the bread crumbs in a medium mixing bowl. Drop by heaping tablespoons onto a hot non-stick skillet. Cook on both sides over low heat until browned. May be frozen.

*You can use frozen vegetables or steam fresh vegetables until tender.

GREENY BEANY CASSEROLE*

With the cheese and whole grains, this is more than just a vegetable dish!

2	tsp. margarine
2	tsp. whole wheat flour
1/3	cup plain yogurt
1	tbsp. grated onion
1/2	lb. fresh green beans, stem ends trimmed and cut into 1 1/2-inch pieces
1/4	cup grated cheddar cheese
2	tbsp. fine dry whole wheat bread crumbs
1	tsp. margarine, melted

Preheat oven to 350°. Cook the 2 tsp. margarine and flour in a medium non-stick skillet over medium heat until bubbly, stirring constantly. Add the yogurt and onions. Remove from heat and add the green beans. Transfer to a shallow 1/2–1 quart casserole dish. Sprinkle with cheese. Combine the bread crumbs and margarine and sprinkle over the cheese. Cover and bake for 40 minutes or until beans are tender. Cool and serve. May be frozen.

*For toddlers with molars.

WHAT A WORK OF ARTICHOKE!*

Now that my children are older, they appreciate a whole artichoke and are pretty adept at eating it on their own. Until your toddler reaches that point, this is a delicious way for him to appreciate the flavor.

1	tsp. vegetable oil
1	tbsp. onion, finely chopped
1	small clove garlic
½	package frozen artichoke hearts, defrosted, drained and chopped
1	small apple, peeled, cored and finely chopped
¾	cup fine dry whole wheat bread crumbs
½	cup shredded cheddar cheese
1	tsp. fresh chopped parsley
2	eggs, beaten

Preheat oven to 350°. Heat the oil in a medium non-stick skillet over medium heat. Add the onion and garlic. Sauté until lightly browned. Remove from heat. Add all other ingredients except the eggs. Transfer to a medium mixing bowl and add the eggs. Spread evenly into a greased 1 quart square or rectangular casserole dish. Bake 25–30 minutes. Allow to cool and cut into squares. May be frozen.

*For toddlers with molars.

MY LITTLE SPROUT*

Brussels sprouts are high in vitamin C and to my knowledge not available in baby food jars!

5   oz. single serving box frozen brussels sprouts
2   tbsp. light cream cheese
1   tbsp. milk
½   tsp. prepared mustard
¼   tsp. lemon juice

Cook sprouts according to package directions. Cut larger sprouts into halves or quarters.

In a small saucepan, cook the remaining ingredients over low heat just until combined. Pour over sprouts and toss. Cool and serve. May be frozen.

*For toddlers with molars.

PETER RABBIT JIGGLER

Your baby will love the way these veggies jiggle!

1   envelope unflavored gelatin
1   cup hot milk
3   oz. cream cheese
2   tsp. lemon juice
1   cup sliced carrots (approximately 2 medium)
1   cup peeled, cored and diced apple
     (approximately 1 small)
¼   cup watercress

In a blender or food processor process the gelatin and milk for 30 seconds. Add the cream cheese and lemon juice and process 10 seconds. Add the carrot, watercress, and apple and grind for 20 seconds or until thoroughly pureed. Turn into an 8-inch square or loaf pan and chill until firm. Cut into squares and serve.

PEAS AND CARROT BALLS

Okay, your toddler can eat cooked peas and carrots together anytime—but isn't this just a little more fun!

2   small carrots, grated
1   tbsp. minced onion
2   tbsp. margarine
1   large egg, beaten
1   cup frozen unsalted peas, defrosted, drained, and processed in a blender or food processor until lightly chopped
³/₄   cup matzo meal
    dash pepper

Cook the carrots and onion in 1 tbsp. of the margarine in a non-stick skillet over medium heat for 10 minutes or until very tender. Remove to a medium mixing bowl and cool. Add the egg, peas, ½ cup of the matzo meal and pepper. Roll into small ½-inch balls and coat with remaining matzo meal.

Heat the remaining margarine in the non-stick skillet over low-medium heat. Add the balls to skillet and cover. Cook until browned on all sides, stirring often. Cool and serve whole or cut up. May be frozen.

CAULIFLOWER AU GRATIN

Try this sauce with other veggies too!

2   slices American cheese
1   tbsp. margarine
1–2 tbsp. cold milk
2   tsp. cornstarch
1   cup cauliflower flowerets
    (washed and steamed until tender)

Melt cheese and margarine in small saucepan over low heat. Stir cornstarch into the milk and add to cheese, stirring constantly until mixture is smooth. Pour over cauliflower and serve.

CAULIFLOWER PARMESAN

This works just as well with broccoli and it's so simple!

1   cup cauliflower flowerets
    (washed and steamed until tender)
1   tbsp. margarine, melted
1   tbsp. Parmesan cheese

Place cauliflower in a bowl and toss with the margarine and Parmesan then serve.

SPICED UP CARROTS

Carrots, because of their naturally sweet flavor, are usually well received by babies. This spiced up version is sure to be a hit!

1	tbsp. margarine
2	tbsp. unsweetened pineapple juice concentrate
¼	tsp. cinnamon
	dash nutmeg
1	cup ¼-inch thick carrot rounds, steamed until tender

Melt the margarine in a small saucepan over low heat. Add the pineapple juice concentrate, cinnamon and nutmeg. Stir until combined and add the carrots. Remove from heat and toss to coat.

6

Pancakes

When you think "pancakes," you probably conjure up an image of a fluffy, golden cake mountain, soaked in a pound of butter with a volcanic flow of caramel-colored syrup running down the sides. While this sounds yummy—let's face it—it's not something a baby should be eating (nor an adult for that matter!). You may as well sit down to a meal of candy bars and chocolate chip cookies! Pancakes are usually lacking in nutritional value, yet, for many, they are a breakfast staple.

The recipes I have devised are still fun to eat but are intended to be eaten without sugary toppings. It's no wonder children of all ages love pancakes. If you put maple syrup over broccoli they'd probably love that too! When a pancake is meant to be sweet, I have "built in" the sweetness, but don't expect all of these to be sweet! Some are even made with vegetables or rice! They all have their own unique flavor and can play any part of a meal—main dish, side dish or dessert.

Babies love their texture and subtle taste, and parents love the fact that they freeze so well and defrost easily in a microwave or toaster.

Speaking of texture, I have used whole wheat flour in all of the recipes, but for a chewier texture (or if your child is allergic to wheat), you may substitute oat flour for all or part of the wheat flour. (See Chapter 2 on how to make your own.)

Try all of these pancake recipes, and see why they earned a chapter all to themselves!

NANA PANCAKES

Babies usually love the taste of bananas, so you can't go wrong by cooking up a batch of these!

½   cup whole wheat flour
½   tsp. baking powder
1   small ripe banana
1   small egg, beaten
⅓   cup milk, breast milk or formula
1   tsp. vegetable oil

Stir flour and baking powder together in a medium mixing bowl. Set aside.

In a small bowl combine the banana, egg, milk and oil. Add to flour mixture, stirring just until blended, but slightly lumpy. Drop by tablespoons onto preheated non-stick griddle or skillet. Cook over medium-low heat until edges are crisp and center is bubbly. Flip over with spatula and brown other sides. May be frozen.

FRUIGURT PANCAKES

Who needs syrup?! These taste so yummy, you'll never miss it!

1   egg
1   tbsp. vegetable oil
1   cup whole wheat flour
1/2   cup fruit juice sweetened yogurt
1/4   cup milk, breast milk or formula
2   tbsp. 100% fruit juice concentrate
     (mixed, apple, pineapple, etc.)
1/8   tsp. baking soda

In a medium mixing bowl, beat together egg and oil. Add the flour, yogurt, milk, fruit juice concentrate and baking soda. Beat until just combined (batter will be thick and smooth).

Drop batter by tablespoons onto a hot non-stick skillet or griddle. Cook on both sides until golden over medium-low heat. Serve whole or cut in pieces. May be frozen.

KIDDIE CREPES

These can also be spread with cream cheese or peanut butter diluted with milk.

1   egg yolk
1/2   cup cottage cheese
1/2   cup unsweetened applesauce
1/2   cup whole wheat flour
1   egg white, stiffly beaten
     100% fruit spread (optional)

Combine egg yolk, cottage cheese, applesauce and flour. Fold in egg white. Drop by heaping tablespoons onto preheated non-stick griddle or skillet. Flatten with back of spoon, then fry on both sides over low heat until cooked through. Allow to cool.

Roll up like a jelly roll and serve plain, or spread a dollop of 100% fruit spread over top and roll up like a fruit crepe. May be frozen.

CORNY BLUE CAKES

Your child will like them for the color but love them for the taste!

³/₄	cup cornmeal
³/₄	cup boiling water
¹/₄	cup whole wheat flour
¹/₂	tsp. baking soda
1	egg, beaten
¹/₂	cup + 2 tbsp. buttermilk
¹/₂	cup blueberries
1	tbsp. whole wheat flour

Combine the cornmeal and boiling water in a medium mixing bowl and stir until smooth. Let stand 10 minutes.

In a small bowl combine flour and baking soda.

Stir the beaten egg and buttermilk into the cornmeal until well combined (batter will be slightly lumpy). Add the flour mixture and stir just until combined.

Place the blueberries in a food processor or blender and coarsely chop. Add the 1 tbsp. flour and stir to coat. Add to the cornmeal batter and gently stir.

Preheat a large non-stick griddle or skillet over medium heat. Drop heaping tablespoons of batter onto skillet and cook on both sides until lightly browned. Cool and serve whole or cut in pieces. May be frozen.

JOHNNY APPLESEED CAKES

These are a great first finger food. Most babies have already been started on apple juice and/or applesauce so the flavor is familiar to them.

2   small apples, peeled, cored and diced
2   eggs
3   tbsp. milk, breast milk or formula
2   tbsp. apple juice concentrate
1/2 cup whole wheat flour
1/4 tsp. cinnamon

In a food processor or blender, process the apples, eggs, milk and apple juice concentrate until blended but thick. Pour into a medium mixing bowl. Add the flour and cinnamon to the wet ingredients. Stir just until combined.

Preheat a large non-stick griddle or skillet over medium heat. Drop the apple batter by tablespoons onto griddle and cook on both sides until browned. Cool and serve whole or in pieces. May be frozen.

FRUIT AND CHEESE CAKES

The fruit gives them sweetness and the cheese and milk provide protein. What a great combo!

$1/2$–$3/4$ cup whole wheat flour
1   tsp. baking powder
1   egg
1   small apple, peeled, cored and cubed
$1/2$ cup shredded cheddar cheese
$1/4$ cup milk
2   tbsp. apple juice concentrate

In a medium mixing bowl, combine $1/2$ cup whole wheat flour and baking powder. Set aside.

Place remaining ingredients in a food processor or blender. Blend until apple is mushy. Pour into flour mixture all at once. Stir until blended but slightly lumpy. Add more flour if batter is too thin.

Preheat non-stick griddle or skillet over medium heat. Pour batter by tablespoons onto hot griddle and cook on both sides until browned. Cool and serve whole or in pieces. May be frozen.

PUMPKIN PIE PANCAKES

Instead of reaching for that pumpkin pie on Thanksgiving, give your baby this special treat!

$1/2$ cup whole wheat flour
1   tsp. baking soda
$1/2$ cup canned unsweetened pumpkin
$1/2$ cup milk, breast milk or formula
3   tbsp. apple juice concentrate
$1/4$ tsp. ginger
$1/4$ tsp. cinnamon
$1/4$ tsp. nutmeg

In a small bowl combine the flour and baking soda. Set aside.

In a medium mixing bowl, stir together the pumpkin, milk, the apple juice concentrate and the spices. Add the flour mixture to pumpkin and stir just until combined.

Preheat a large non-stick griddle or skillet over low heat. Pour the batter by tablespoons onto griddle and cook on both sides until browned. Cool and serve whole or in pieces. May be frozen.

TOFRUITY PANCAKE

The tofu makes these pancakes extra moist.

3/4   cup whole wheat flour
1/2   tsp. baking powder
1   egg
5   oz. soft tofu, drained
1/2   cup milk, breast milk or formula
4   tbsp. apple juice concentrate
1   tsp. vegetable oil
1/2   tsp. vanilla

In a small bowl combine the flour and baking powder. Set aside.

Put all remaining ingredients in a blender or food processor. Process until combined and poured into a medium mixing bowl. Add flour mixture and stir until smooth.

Preheat a large non-stick griddle or skillet over medium heat. Pour batter by tablespoons onto hot skillet and cook on both sides until browned. Cool and serve whole or in pieces. May be frozen.

MARTIAN NUGGETS

The green color looks so fun to eat; they'll never guess it's good for them! These are also great for snacks so make a big batch!

½ cup *finely* grated zucchini
     (approximately 1 small)
⅓ cup whole wheat flour
¼ cup grated Parmesan cheese
1 egg, beaten
2 tbsp. grated onion
1 tsp. dried parsley flakes

Mix all ingredients together in a medium mixing bowl.

Preheat non-stick griddle or skillet over medium-low heat. Drop batter by heaping teaspoons onto skillet. Brown on both sides. Cool and serve. May be frozen.

ONE POTATO, TWO POTATO ...

In the Jewish tradition, these are called Latkes. I decided to sneak in the sweet potato, but you can make them the traditional way with white potatoes only. They are delicious with applesauce or sour cream!

1 medium unpeeled white rose potato
1 small unpeeled sweet potato
1 egg
½ small onion
2 tbsp. whole wheat flour or matzo meal
½ tsp. garlic powder

Scrub and quarter both potatoes. Puree all ingredients in a food processor or strong blender* until near smooth (no potato lumps). Drop by tablespoons onto hot non-stick skillet and flatten with the back of spoon. Brown approximately 3 minutes on each side over low heat. Cool and serve whole or in pieces. May be frozen.

*You may also grate the potatoes and onion and then mix with remaining ingredients.

RICE CAKES

No, these aren't the tasteless rice cakes that you buy at the store! These actually taste good and contain fiber to boot!

1   egg
1   cup buttermilk
³/₄   cup whole wheat flour
¹/₂   tsp. baking soda
1   cup soft cooked brown rice
      (approximately ¹/₂ cup uncooked)
1   tbsp. margarine

Beat the egg with a wire whisk until frothy in a medium mixing bowl. Beat in buttermilk. Set aside.

In a small bowl combine the flour and baking soda. Add flour mixture to egg mixture, beating constantly. Add the rice and margarine.

Preheat a large non-stick griddle or skillet over medium-low heat. Pour batter by tablespoons onto skillet and brown on both sides. Serve whole or in pieces. May be frozen.

FALAFEL FRITTERS

If Mom or Dad want to go "Mediterranean" too, put a couple of these into pita bread with sliced cucumber and Tahini sauce or mayonnaise.

7	oz. cooked chickpeas, rinsed and drained
1	egg
1/4	cup whole wheat flour
2	tbsp. chopped fresh parsley
1	tbsp. chopped onion
1	scallion, roughly chopped
1	small clove garlic, slivered
2	tsp. olive oil
	dash pepper

Process all ingredients in a food processor or blender until almost smooth.

Preheat a large non-stick skillet over medium heat. Drop by tablespoons onto skillet. Brown both sides, flattening slightly with spatula. Cool and serve whole or in pieces. May be frozen.

7

Breads, Muffins, Cakes and Snacks

I'm sure it seems like yesterday when you brought your baby home from the hospital to find that all she did was eat and sleep. It probably seemed like her every waking moment was spent with a nipple in her mouth. This wasn't your imagination!

As your baby's stomach grew and she began solids, her feedings most likely became less frequent. But it will be well into the future before your child can eat 3 meals a day. Babies and toddlers need to snack throughout the day. Their tummies are still too small to hold enough food to sustain them to the next meal—especially the traditional 3 meals a day. Mealtimes and snacktimes may become a blur because your baby will seem to be "grazing" all day. After your baby's first birthday, when her growth rate slows down and she requires less food, it may seem as if she is barely eating enough to survive.

With this in mind, everything babies put in their little mouths should be nutritious. Every time you give your baby a sugar filled cookie, you are taking up the very limited space in her belly where a banana or something more healthful could have gone.

To babies and toddlers, snacks are not just what the name implies, but a major part of their diet. All of these recipes are filled with nutrition and though they still taste like treats, you can be assured that your child is not getting one empty calorie.

WHOLE GRAIN BREAD

With breadmakers becoming so popular, it's easier than ever to make your own! Try this one!

1   package active dry yeast
1¼ cups of warm water
3   cups whole wheat flour or combination of
      whole wheat and oat flour
3   tbsp. wheat gluten*
2   tbsp. apple juice concentrate
2   tbsp. margarine

Dissolve the yeast in 1¼ cups warm water in a large bowl. Add 1½ cups flour, wheat gluten, apple juice concentrate, and margarine. Beat with an electric mixer on medium speed for about 2 minutes. Add the remaining 1½ cups flour. Beat with a spoon and then knead with your hands 1–1½ minutes. Cover and let rise in a warm place (an oven that is shut off is a good place) for about 45 minutes or until it doubles in size.

Knead batter about 25 times and press into a greased 9-inch loaf pan. Pat smooth with floured hands. Allow to rise about 45 minutes.

Heat oven to 375°. Bake for 45–50 minutes or

until loaf is browned. Cool on wire rack before cutting.

*You can usually find this in the "baking needs" section of a grocery store. If not, then a health food store will carry it.

SWEET BROWN BREAD

The dried fruits in this sweet bread make it a good source of iron.

¼ cup apple juice concentrate
¼ cup water
½ cup pitted dates, chopped fine
½ cup pitted dried figs, chopped fine
1½ tbsp. margarine
1½ tsp. baking soda
1 egg
¾ cup whole wheat flour
¼ tsp. baking powder

In a small saucepan, bring the apple juice concentrate and water to a boil. Meanwhile, in a medium mixing bowl, combine the dates, figs, margarine and baking soda. Pour the boiling apple juice mixture into the date mixture and stir until well combined. Allow to sit for about 15 minutes.

Preheat oven to 350°. Beat the egg into the date and fig mixture. In a small bowl stir together the flour and baking powder. Add to the wet ingredients and beat just until blended. Pour into 1–2 (depending on size) greased and floured mini loaf pans about ¾ full. Place on a cookie sheet and bake 40–50 minutes or until toothpick inserted into centers comes out clean. Cool for 10 minutes and remove from pans onto a wire rack. Cool completely and cut into slices. May be frozen.

APRICOT, SPICE AND EVERYTHING NICE LOAVES

Spice up your baby's diet with these tasty little loaves!

1	large egg
1	small banana, cut into chunks
1	cup chopped dried unsweetened apricots
1/3	cup apple juice
2	tbsp. vegetable oil
1	tsp. vanilla
1	cup whole wheat flour
1	tsp. baking powder
1/2	tsp. baking soda
1/2	tsp. allspice

Preheat oven to 325°. In a blender or food processor, combine the egg, banana, apricots, apple juice, oil and vanilla. Process until almost smooth and pour into a bowl.

In a small bowl combine the flour, baking powder, baking soda and allspice. Add to the apricot mixture and stir well.

Pour into 2–3 (depending on size) greased and floured mini loaf pans. Bake for 30–35 minutes or until toothpick inserted in centers comes out clean. Allow to cool for 10 minutes and remove from pans to a wire rack. Cool completely before slicing. May be frozen.

WHAT A NUT CAKE!

This non-sweet cake has a little of everything in it!

³/₄ cup pecan halves
½ cup diced carrot (approximately 1 medium)
³/₄ cup milk, breast milk or formula
2 tbsp. chopped onion
1 small egg
¼ cup whole wheat flour
½ cup American cheese
  (approximately 4 slices), torn
½ cup wheat germ

In a blender or food processor add the pecans, carrot, milk, onion and egg. Process until smooth. Pour into a medium saucepan. Add the flour. Cook over low heat, stirring constantly, until thickened. Remove from heat.

Add the cheese and wheat germ. Stir until cheese melts. Spread into 2–3 (depending on size) greased and floured mini loaf pans about ³/₄ full. Bake in a 350° oven 50 minutes or until knife inserted in centers comes out clean. Cool for 10 minutes on a wire rack and remove from pans. Allow to cool completely before slicing. May be frozen.

PUMPKIN MUFFINS

Muffins freeze well and are easy to defrost in the microwave. Great for an "on the go" breakfast!

1	cup whole wheat flour
1	tsp. baking powder
$1/2$	tsp. cinnamon
$1/8$	tsp. nutmeg
1	cup unsweetened solid packed pumpkin
6	oz. apple juice concentrate
2	tbsp. milk, breast milk or formula
1	tbsp. vegetable oil
1	egg
$1/4$	cup raisins
$1/4$	cup chopped dates

Preheat oven to 375°. Mix the flour, baking powder, cinnamon and nutmeg in a medium mixing bowl and set aside.

Place all remaining ingredients in a blender or food processor. Puree until smooth and dates and raisins are completely chopped. Add to flour mixture and stir until well combined.

Spoon into a 12-cup greased muffin tin. Bake for about 20 minutes or until toothpick inserted in center of muffins comes out clean. Let cool 5 minutes, and remove from pan. Cool on a wire rack. May be frozen.

KIWI-PEAR MUFFINS

The whole family will enjoy snacking on these!

½	cup whole wheat flour
¼	cup wheat germ
1	tsp. baking powder
¼	tsp. nutmeg
¾	cup fresh cubed very ripe pear, skin and seeds removed
2	very ripe medium kiwis, skin removed
½	cup chopped dates
1	egg

Preheat oven to 350°. In a medium mixing bowl combine flour, wheat germ, baking powder and nutmeg. Set aside.

In a blender or food processor place the pear, kiwis, dates and egg. Puree until smooth. Add to dry ingredients and mix well. Pour evenly into a 6-cup greased muffin tin. Bake for 25–30 minutes or until toothpick inserted in middle of muffins comes out clean and tops are browned. Cool on wire rack. May be frozen.

LITTLE MISS MUFFIN

A basic muffin that toddlers love!

1	small egg
1	tbsp. vegetable oil
¾	cup unsweetened applesauce
½	cup raisins
1	cup whole wheat flour
1	tsp. baking powder
½	tsp. baking soda
¼	tsp. nutmeg
¼	tsp. cinnamon

Preheat oven to 375°. In a blender or food processor place the egg, vegetable oil, applesauce and raisins. Process until raisins are chopped. Pour into a medium mixing bowl.

In a small bowl combine the remaining dry ingredients. Add to the applesauce mixture. Stir until blended. Evenly distribute batter into a greased 6-cup muffin tin. Bake for 20–25 minutes or until firm and brown. Cool on wire rack. May be frozen.

BAKED SWEET SPUDUMPLINGS

Tastes like a sweet potato pie—without the sugar!

1	cup whole wheat flour
1/4	cup mashed sweet potato
2	tsp. baking powder
3	tbsp. margarine
3	tbsp. milk, breast milk or formula
2	tbsp. apple juice concentrate

Preheat oven to 400°. In a medium mixing bowl, mix together the flour, sweet potato and baking powder. Cut in the margarine. Stir in the milk and concentrate.

Drop by tablespoons onto an ungreased cookie sheet. Bake 12–15 minutes or until browned. May be frozen.

BARLEY KUGEL

Barley has a great texture that older babies usually love.

2	cups water
1/2	cup pearl barley
1	tsp. margarine
1/4	lb. chopped mushrooms
1	tbsp. minced onion
	dash pepper
2	eggs, beaten

Bring the water to a boil in a medium saucepan. Stir in the barley. Lower heat, cover and simmer for 45 minutes or until barley is soft and water is absorbed.

In a medium non-stick skillet melt the margarine. Add the mushrooms and onions. Cook until limp and browned. Add the barley and pepper. Remove from heat and allow to cool slightly. Stir in the eggs. Spread evenly into a greased 1 quart baking dish.

Bake in a 350° oven 30 minutes or until browned and set. Cool and cut into squares. May be frozen.

SCONES

Light and fluffy scones made with whole grains? You bet! And, babies gobble them up!

3/4	cup whole wheat flour
1/4	cup rolled oats
1	tsp. cream of tartar
1/2	tsp. baking soda
3	tbsp. margarine
1/4	cup fresh raisins, chopped *finely*
1/4	cup milk, breast milk or formula

Preheat oven to 350°. In a medium mixing bowl combine the flour, oats, cream of tartar and baking soda. Cut in the margarine. Add the raisins and mix well. Stir in the milk until dough can be made into a ball.

Transfer to a floured surface and roll out until ½ inch thick. Cut into circles with a biscuit cutter (or use a cookie cutter for fun shapes!). Place on an ungreased cookie sheet and bake until browned 10–15 minutes. May be frozen.

WEE WILLIE WAFFLES

Spread a little margarine and/or fruit juice sweetened jam on top of these while they are still warm—yum!

¾	cup whole wheat flour
¼	cup yellow cornmeal
¼	cup wheat germ
1	tsp. baking powder
½	tsp. baking soda
½	tsp. nutmeg
1	egg
¾	cup buttermilk
3	tbsp. apple juice concentrate
2	tbsp. vegetable oil
½	cup chopped raisins

In a small mixing bowl mix together the flour, cornmeal, wheat germ, baking powder, baking soda and nutmeg. Set aside.

In a medium mixing bowl whisk together the egg, buttermilk, apple juice concentrate and oil. Add the raisins and stir well.

Heat waffle iron. Brush lightly with vegetable oil

if necessary. Add the flour mixture to the batter and stir just until combined. Pour about 1 cup batter onto iron and spread to edges. Bring top down and cook 4–6 minutes or until browned. May be frozen and reheated in toaster or oven.

MATZO BALLS SANS SOUP

Substitute the water for chicken stock and you have a soup the whole family can enjoy. Remove the matzo balls with a slotted spoon for baby.

2　　eggs
2　　tbsp. apple juice concentrate
1　　tbsp. unsweetened applesauce
2　　tsp. oil
½　　cup matzo meal

Beat the eggs, apple juice concentrate, applesauce and oil together in a medium mixing bowl. Add matzo meal and stir until well combined. Cover and refrigerate for 15 minutes.

Bring 1½ quarts of water to a boil. Roll matzo mixture into 1-inch balls with wet hands. Cover, and without lifting lid, boil for 35 minutes. Remove with slotted spoon. May be frozen.

CHEWY GOOEY COOKIES

These aren't as messy as they sound!

1/2	cup oats
1/2	cup whole wheat flour
1/2	tsp. baking powder
1/4	cup raisins
1/4	cup chopped dates
1	small very ripe banana
1/3	cup sugar- and salt-free peanut butter
1/4	cup milk, breast milk or formula
1/4	tsp. vanilla
1	egg

In a medium mixing bowl combine oats, flour and baking powder. Set aside.

In a blender or food processor place raisins, dates, banana, peanut butter, milk, vanilla and egg. Puree until smooth. Add to flour mixture. Drop by tablespoons onto non-stick ungreased baking sheet. Bake for 10–12 minutes or until browned on bottom. Cool on wire rack. Store in an airtight container in refrigerator or freezer.

FRUITY COOKIES

With cookies like these, who needs the sugar filled variety?!

1/4   cup chopped dried unsweetened apricots
1/4   cup raisins
1/4   cup chopped dates
1/2   cup orange juice concentrate
1   small egg
2   tbsp. unsweetened applesauce
1   tbsp. vegetable oil
3/4   cup oats
1/2   cup whole wheat flour
1/2   tsp. baking soda

Preheat oven to 350°. Combine apricots, raisins, dates and orange juice concentrate in a small non-stick saucepan. Simmer 5–10 minutes over low heat, stirring often, until fruit is tender. Remove from heat and allow to cool.

Transfer to a blender or food processor. Add the egg, applesauce and oil. Blend until fruit is pureed. Transfer to a medium mixing bowl.

In a small bowl, mix together the oats, flour and baking soda. Add to fruit mixture. Drop by tea-spoons on an ungreased cookie sheet. Bake for 10 minutes or until browned. Store in an airtight container in refrigerator or freezer.

FRUIT CAKE

I'm happy to say that this is not your traditional fruit cake!

1	egg white
1/3	cup whole wheat flour
1	tsp. baking powder
1	egg yolk
1	ripe banana, mashed
2	tbsp. unsweetened fruit juice concentrate (apple, pineapple, mixed, etc.)
1	cup finely chopped fresh fruit such as peaches, pears, kiwis, etc.

Preheat oven and cookie sheet to 350°. Beat the egg white in a small bowl until stiff and set aside. Combine the flour and baking powder in another small bowl and set aside. In a large mixing bowl beat together the egg yolk, banana and fruit juice concentrate. Stir in the chopped fruit.

Add the flour mixture to the fruit mixture and then gently fold in the egg white. Spoon into 2–3 (depending on size) greased and floured miniature loaf pans about 3/4 full.

Bake on cookie sheet in oven for 25–30 minutes or until set and browned. Allow to cool, remove from pans and slice. May be frozen.

PETER RABBIT CAKE

My baby and I love to share this for breakfast, warmed and spread with cream cheese or butter!

2   small eggs
¼   cup soft margarine
½   cup apple juice concentrate
1¼   cups whole wheat flour
1   tsp. baking powder
½   tsp. baking soda
½   tsp. nutmeg
½   tsp. cinnamon
1½   cups grated carrot

Grease and flour an 8-inch loaf pan. Preheat oven to 350°. In a medium mixing bowl, beat together the eggs, margarine and apple juice concentrate. In a small bowl mix together the flour, baking powder, baking soda, nutmeg and cinnamon. Add to egg mixture and beat until well combined. Stir in grated carrot.

Spread batter into the prepared loaf pan. Bake for 25–30 minutes or until browned and set. Cool on wire rack. Slice and serve.

· PRUNICOT CAKE

This cake is a must for any baby who suffers from constipation!

1	cup whole wheat flour
1/4	cup wheat germ
1	tsp. baking powder
1/2	tsp. cinnamon
1/2	tsp. nutmeg
1/4	tsp. baking soda
1	large egg
1/2	cup fruit sweetened yogurt
1/3	cup chopped pitted prunes*
1/3	cup chopped pitted dried unsweetened apricots*
1/4	cup unsweetened applesauce
1	tbsp. vegetable oil

Preheat oven to 375°. Stir together the flour, wheat germ, baking powder, cinnamon, nutmeg and baking soda in a small mixing bowl. Set aside.

In a blender or food processor, process the remaining ingredients until smooth. Pour into a medium mixing bowl. Add the flour mixture and stir just until blended.

Spread into 2–3 (depending on size) greased and floured mini loaf pans about 3/4 full. Bake for 20 minutes or until toothpick in center of loaves comes out clean. Cool and cut into slices. May be frozen.

*If you are using a food processor, there is no need to chop first.

CHERUB'S CHEESECAKE PUFFS

I have to get these into the freezer right away because I have a tendency to eat them before my daughter even gets a bite!

1   large egg, separated
1/2   cup ricotta or cottage cheese
1/4   cup instant nonfat dry milk
1/2   small very ripe banana
2   tbsp. fruit juice sweetened yogurt, stirred
2   tsp. whole wheat flour
1/2   tsp. lemon juice
1/2   tsp. vanilla extract

Preheat oven to 400°. Beat the egg white in a small mixing bowl until stiff. Set aside.

In a blender or food processor whip all remaining ingredients. Pour into a medium mixing bowl. Gently fold in the egg white.

Pour into a 6-cup greased and floured muffin tin about 2/3 full each. Bake for 15–20 minutes or until firm in the center. Cool and remove from pan. May be frozen.

BANANUTTY SANDWICH

Peanut butter and banana taste so good together! If you don't believe me try this recipe!

1   tbsp. smooth sugar- and salt-free peanut butter
1/2   small ripe banana
2   slices whole wheat bread
1   tbsp. margarine

In a small bowl mash together the peanut butter and banana until combined and peanut butter is thinned. Spread on 1 slice of bread and cover with other slice to make a sandwich. Spread the outsides of the sandwich with the margarine and cook in a non-stick skillet over medium-low heat on both sides until lightly browned. Cool and cut into quarters to serve.

ALMOND JIGGLES

A different twist on the already popular gelatin squares. This recipe has added calcium and protein!

1   envelope unflavored gelatin
½   cup water
1   cup milk, breast milk or formula
1   cup apple juice concentrate
2   tsp. almond extract
¼   cup slivered almonds,
       chopped or crushed into a rough powder

Sprinkle gelatin over the water to soften. Heat the milk and apple juice concentrate until hot in a microwave or saucepan. Add the gelatin/water mixture and stir until dissolved. Add the almond extract and almonds. Pour mixture into a shallow 8-inch square pan and refrigerate until firm. Cut into squares.

JUICE JIGGLES

This recipe is always a favorite! It is a little less messy to eat if you exclude the peaches.

2   cups unsweetened fruit juice
2   envelopes unflavored gelatin
½   cup diced peaches in their own juice, drained

Mix ½ cup cold juice and gelatin in a large bowl. Heat the remaining 1½ cups juice until boiling. Pour into gelatin mixture and stir until all gelatin is dissolved. Add diced peaches. Pour into an 8-inch square pan and chill until set. Cut into squares.

WHAT A PEAR!

This is a great way to use pears that are too hard for your baby to eat uncooked.

1   pear, peeled, cored and quartered
2   tbsp. unsweetened fruit juice concentrate
⅛   tsp. cinnamon

Preheat oven to 350°. Place pear in an individual casserole dish. Heat the fruit juice concentrate and cinnamon in a microwave or saucepan until bubbly. Pour over pear. Bake, uncovered, for 10 minutes. Turn pear over and bake 10 more minutes. Cool and serve in quarters or cut into chunks.

PINEAPPLE BALLS

My daughter liked these with pineapple, but you can use any fruit that your child favors. Make sure that you get the dried fruit without sugar.

½ an 8 oz. can of crushed pineapple
  in its own juice, drained
1 8 oz. package cream cheese
¼ cup dried pineapple or apricots,
  ground in a food processor or blender

Mash all ingredients together—go ahead use your hands! Roll into 1-inch balls and serve. Keeps in the refrigerator for as long as the cream cheese is fresh (check the date on the package).

BRAN CRACKLES

High in fiber—these are definitely not just an empty snack!

½ cup apple juice or other unsweetened juice
½ cup bran
½ cup whole wheat flour
¼ cup nonfat dry milk
1 tsp. cinnamon
¼ tsp. cloves
1 egg
1 tbsp. vegetable oil

Preheat oven to 350°. Bring the juice to a boil in medium saucepan. Meanwhile combine the bran, flour, milk and spices. Stir into the juice and remove from heat. Beat in the egg until well combined. Form into two logs and slice an ⅛ inch thick. Rub oil over two pans and arrange the slices, flattening them on the pans. Bake for 10–15 minutes or until crisp. Store in an airtight container.

BABY'S BREAD STICKS

A great accompaniment with any meal or just as a snack to carry in the diaper bag. This recipe can easily be doubled or tripled once you have tested it.

1 slice whole wheat bread
2 tsp. margarine, softened
2 tsp. Parmesan cheese

Preheat oven to 375°. Combine the margarine and Parmesan together with a fork. Spread over the bread. Cut bread into sticks about ½ inch thick. Place in single layer on baking sheet. Bake for 5–10 minutes or until crisp.

8

Drinks and Frozen Snacks

Although drinks may not be considered a finger food, I have included them because all but one can be frozen and then, voilà—instant finger food! What could feel (or taste!) better to a teething baby than a nice cold frozen treat? And, since many teething babies lose their appetites, this is a great way to get some nutrition into their bellies! To freeze these drinks, simply pour into a paper cup, cover with aluminum foil, poke a popsicle stick through the center and place in the freezer. If you'd like to reblend back into a drink, place in a blender or food processor and add enough liquid (preferably a liquid already in the recipe) to blend into a slushy treat.

The shakes and thicker drinks are great for beginning cup users because they "roll" slowly into the mouth as opposed to splashing all over the face! The more fluid drinks may be put in a baby bottle or training cup.

The drinks containing milk and/or yogurt are perfect for babies on a "milk boycott." They're so yummy, they'll never guess you've slipped them a "protein disguise!"

Whichever way you choose to serve them, these drinks are sure to be a hit with the entire family!

BAA BAA BLACK SHAKE

A delicious way for your baby to drink some fiber!

¼   cup milk, breast milk or formula
2   tbsp. raisins
3–5 ice cubes

Blend all ingredients together in a food processor or blender using ice cubes according to desired thickness. Check for ice chunks before serving. May be frozen.

BRANDON'S SHAKE

I have to give my son credit for this one since he invented it!

1   ripe banana
½   cup plain yogurt
½   cup unsweetened fruit juice
     fresh fruit such as blueberries, peaches,
     pears, etc.

Blend all ingredients in a food processor or blender until smooth. Add fresh fruit according to taste.

GARRETT'S SHAKE

I asked my younger son to put his favorite ingredients in a drink, and this is what he came up with!

¼ slice of a ripe cantaloupe, cut into chunks
¼ cup peach flavored, fruit juice
     sweetened yogurt
¼ cup milk, breast milk or formula
3–5 ice cubes

Blend all ingredients in a food processor or blender using ice according to desired thickness. Check for ice chunks before serving. May be frozen.

BERRY, BERRY GOOD SHAKE!

This creamy drink is sure to be a hit!

½ cup frozen berries such as blueberries,
     strawberries, etc.
¼ cup berry flavored, fruit juice
     sweetened yogurt
¼ cup milk, breast milk or formula

While fruit is frozen, blend together with yogurt and milk in a food processor or blender. Drink immediately. May be frozen.

HEALTHY BABY SHAKE

They will never know the wheat germ is in there!

¼ cup milk, breast milk or formula
2 tbsp. unsweetened fruit juice concentrate
2 tsp. wheat germ
3–4 ice cubes

Blend all ingredients in a food processor or blender using ice according to desired thickness. Check for ice chunks before serving. May be frozen.

PEANUT BUTTER AND JELLY SHAKE

It's like a sandwich in a cup!

½   cup milk, breast milk or formula
½   small ripe banana
2   tbsp. sugar- and salt-free peanut butter
1   tbsp. 100% fruit spread

Blend all ingredients in a food processor or blender until smooth. May be frozen.

MELON BALL

Cantaloupe is one of the healthiest fruits you can eat. Serve this drink often.

¼   slice of a small ripe cantaloupe,
     cut into chunks
¼   cup vanilla flavored, fruit juice
     sweetened yogurt
½   tsp. almond extract

Blend all ingredients in a food processor or blender until smooth. May be frozen.

EENSIE WEENSIE CIDER

This is just as bubbly as soda pop but much healthier! Try it with other juices too!

2   tbsp. apple juice concentrate
½   cup low sodium sparkling mineral water

Mix both ingredients in a cup and serve immediately.

FUZZY FRUIT JUICE   ·

This drink is refreshingly frothy! It makes a great fruit "mustache"!

1   cup unsweetened pineapple juice, chilled
½   an orange, peeled, quartered
     and seeds removed
¼   of an apple, cored and sliced
¼   of a pear, cored and sliced

Liquefy all ingredients in a food processor or blender until smooth and frothy. May be frozen.

WHAT A SMOOTHIE!

You can substitute any favorite fruit for the peach.

½   cup cold milk, breast milk or formula
1   peach half, fresh or from an unsweetened can
½   very ripe banana
2   dates
1   tbsp. slivered almond

Blend all ingredients in food processor or blender until smooth and frothy. May be frozen.

BUNNY JUICE

Carrots are surprisingly sweet when made into a juice. There's nothing better for a dose of vitamin A!

½   cup unsweetened pineapple juice, chilled
1   small carrot, sliced

Puree both ingredients in a food processor or blender until smooth. Pour through a strainer into 1–2 cups. Discard ground carrot in strainer. May be frozen.

HUMPTY DUMPTY EGG NOG

This egg nog has no egg, but tastes just as creamy as the real thing!

½   very ripe banana
½   cup chilled milk, breast milk or formula
1   tsp. vanilla extract
½   tsp. nutmeg

Blend all ingredients in a food processor or blender until smooth. May be frozen.

PEACHY COLADA

Cool and refreshing Piña Coladas always remind me of summer. I created this rendition so my children could enjoy them with me.

¾   cup fresh, frozen or canned peaches
     in their own juice, drained
¼   cup unsweetened coconut cream or milk
¼   cup water
¼   cup unsweetened pineapple juice concentrate
3–5 ice cubes

Blend all ingredients in a blender or food processor using ice cubes according to desired thickness. Check for ice chunks before serving. May be frozen.

CREAMSICLE COCKTAIL

Orange and vanilla—an unbeatable combination!

1/2 cup orange juice
1/2 cup fruit juice sweetened vanilla yogurt
1/2 tsp. vanilla
3–5 ice cubes

Blend all ingredients together in a blender or food processor using ice cubes according to desired thickness. Check for ice chunks before serving. May be frozen.

LEMONADE

Regular lemonade is filled with sugar, but who doesn't indulge on a hot day?! Even if you must go for the sugar-filled variety, try to give your baby this one instead.

1/4 cup fresh lemon juice
1 cup orange juice
3/4 cup water
2 tbsp. fruit juice sweetened orange marmalade

Blend all ingredients together in a food processor or blender until smooth and serve. May be frozen.

9

Store-bought
Finger Foods

When I researched this chapter, I realized why this book needed to be written! After visiting many grocery stores, I did manage to come up with a meager list of healthful foods to serve if you don't have the time or energy to cook. Granted, if you visited a health food store, you would find a plethora of healthful foods to choose from, but not all of us are fortunate enough to live near one. So, in keeping with the theme of this book, I have only included items in this list that you will most likely find at your local grocery store.

Remember that it is important to be an ingredient list reader. Even something labeled "all natural" may contain sugar. After all sugar does come from nature so it wouldn't be false advertising! As a general rule, if an ingredient such as salt or sugar is listed fifth or lower on an ingredient list, it is usually only there in small quantities. There are items, though, that have fewer than 5 ingredients, such as Cheerios. In this case you have to look at the grams of sugar (Cheerios only have 1 gram).

I have also formed a list of fruits and vegetables

that you can feed your baby without cooking and without a choking hazard.

Some of the foods I have listed are only a healthful compromise, meaning that they may have traces of either salt, sugar or white flour. Overall, I think they'll do in a pinch!

FRUITS AND VEGETABLES

SOFT RIPE PEARS—skinned, cored and cut into
   slices
GRAPES—cut into tiny pieces
KIWIS—skinned
SOFT RIPE PAPAYA AND MANGO—skinned and
   seeded
SOFT RIPE MELON—cantaloupe, watermelon,
   honeydew, etc.
BERRIES—cut up blueberries, strawberries, rasp-
   berries, etc.
SOFT RIPE PEACHES, PLUMS AND NEC-
   TARINES—peeled and seeded
BANANA—these can also be frozen for teething
   babies
AVOCADOS—peeled and seeded
FROZEN VEGETABLES that are unsalted, such
   as petite peas, chopped broccoli and brussels
   sprouts cut into quarters
CANNED FRUIT IN THEIR OWN JUICE such as
   mandarin oranges, peaches and apricots.

STEAMING FRESH VEGETABLES

Many of the vegetables babies should eat because of their high vitamin and mineral content are also considered choking hazards—especially in their fresh uncooked state.

Fresh vegetables are too important to simply eliminate and the soft mushy veggies in cans are virtually depleted of all their vitamins during the canning process. So how do we make them safe to eat without losing all of their nutritional value? We steam them! A "food steamer" works great but a steam basket is less costly and just as effective.

Some babies refuse to touch vegetables when they are served "au natural" and if that's the case, revert to Chapter 5. But, if you have a veggie lover then get that steamer ready!

As I mentioned before, frozen vegetables will do in a pinch if you don't have time to cook, but when you do, keep in mind that fresh is always best!

To use your "food steamer" refer to your manufacturer's directions on how to cook vegetables. For your steam basket, place enough water in a pot to create steam but not enough to touch the bottom of the basket (about 1 inch). Place small pieces of cut up vegetables into the basket and bring to a boil. Cover the pot and simmer over low heat until the vegetables are very tender and can be cut easily with the side of a fork. As your baby gets older and better at chewing, you can gradually cut down on the steaming time so the vegetables stay firmer and are at less risk of losing their vitamins. Try these vegetables for the best results . . .

Asparagus
Broccoli
Brussels sprouts
Carrots
Cauliflower
Green beans
Peas (shelled)
Spinach
Zucchini

SNACKS

LOW SODIUM WHEAT THINS
LOW SODIUM TRISKETS
WASA CRACKERS—These come in many whole
   grain flavors and are very low sodium.
UNSALTED RICE CAKES
HEALTH VALLEY COOKIES—Most of these are
   fruit juice sweetened, but some do contain
   honey. Read the ingredient lists.
FROOKIE COOKIES—Many flavors to choose
   from and they are all tasty!
HEALTHY OPTIONS COOKIES

BREADS AND CEREALS

WHOLE WHEAT BAGELS—You may have to go to
   a bagel shop for these. ROMAN MEAL is the
   best I could find at the grocery store.
MANISCHEWITZ WHOLE WHEAT MATZO—
   Look in the kosher section for these.

HEALTH VALLEY OAT BRAN O's—Again read
their labels because some contain honey.

HEALTH VALLEY BREAKFAST BARS—Same as
above.

PUFFED WHEAT CEREAL—There are a few
brands of these. Look in the cereal aisle.

NABISCO SPOON SIZE SHREDDED WHEAT—
These contain no sugar or salt; only whole
wheat.

CHEERIOS—Still the old stand-by! Higher than
some cereals in sodium, but it contains whole
grain oat flour and only 1 gram of sugar. A
good compromise and babies usually love them!

PROTEIN FOODS

LOW SODIUM GEFILTE FISH—Look for this in
the kosher aisle.

LA LOMA VEGE-BURGER—Made with no meat
but still very high in protein and relatively low
in sodium. It comes in a can and is usually
located in the diet section.

HOOP CHEESE—This cheese is very low in
sodium which is unusual for cheese and it has
a great soft texture that even toothless babies
will appreciate. Look for it in the gourmet
cheese section.

CONTADINA SPINACH AND 3 CHEESE
TORTELLINI—High in sodium because of the
cheeses but also very high in protein, and it's
easy for babies to pick up!

BROADLEAF'S BUFFALO PATTIES—Buffalo
meat is becoming very popular. It is high in

protein and is naturally tender. These patties are already formed and can be cooked just like a hamburger. Look for it in the specialty meat section.

Postscript

A couple of weeks ago, my 13-year-old son Brandon was thrown from a horse and had to be rushed to the hospital. As I sat in the emergency room awaiting the results of his X-rays (it turned out to be only scrapes and bruises), I realized how unfamiliar hospitals, and doctor's offices in general, were to me. I also came to the realization that my 3 children were probably the healthiest kids I know.

I'm sure Brandon and his 11-year-old brother, Garrett, must have seen the doctor for *something* in the past. However, I can't recall one incident when it was for anything other than routine exams, stitches, or horseback riding fiascos (thankfully, even those have been few and far between!).

Both of them have won numerous attendance awards and, much to their disappointment, have never had anything worse than the sniffles to keep them out of school. And for boys who consider brushing their teeth once a week good dental hygiene, my husband and I are always amazed when they consistently come home from their dental check-ups with no cavities!

My 3-year-old daughter, so far, has the same record. She has had no lingering illnesses, no ear infections and no reasons to bring her into the pediatrician except for her immunizations. I can honestly say that I have never sat on anything other than the "well baby" side of the waiting room! My friends insist this must be some sort of world record!

Am I just the luckiest mother around? Maybe. Is it in their genes? Could be, although my daughter has a different father than my 2 sons—go figure! Has sugar, salt and white flour passed through those healthy lips? Of course! By now all of them have eaten foods that would have made me cringe when I first conceived of these recipes! I have now accepted it as one of those big, bad parts of my children's lives that I can only control when we are together. The difference is that my children *still* like the good foods too. They love fruits, vegetables and whole grains, and they still eat sugar-free cookies!

I will never know if starting them out on these recipes gave them this healthful head start and their appreciation for "fine" foods—it could all be some fantastic coincidence (or just luck!). What I do know is that I did everything in my power to prime their palates for a lifetime of healthy eating *and* healthy living.

Good health to you and yours!

Victoria Jenest and family
May, 1996

Understanding what's happening emotionally and physically as your little one evolves from a baby into a child is a vital part of being an effective parent. In these helpful, down-to-earth guides, you'll learn what to expect and what to do at every stage of development. Filled with caring advice, *The Magical Years* helps you keep up with all of the many changes you'll encounter during this special time in your child's life.

THE MAGICAL YEARS

Janet Poland

GETTING TO KNOW YOUR ONE-YEAR-OLD
_____ 95418-2 $4.99 U.S./$5.99 Can.

SURVIVING YOUR TWO-YEAR-OLD
_____ 95582-0 $4.99 U.S./$5.99 Can.

MAKING FRIENDS WITH YOUR THREE-YEAR-OLD
_____ 95627-4 $4.99 U.S./$5.99 Can.